PAT ROBERTSON: A Warning to America

John W. Robbins

The Trinity Foundation
Jefferson, Maryland 21755

Pat Robertson: A Warning to America
Copyright 1988 John W. Robbins.
All rights reserved.

All quotations from the Bible are from *The King James Version* or *The New King James Version,* copyright 1979, 1980, 1982, 1985, Thomas Nelson, Inc., Nashville, Tennessee.

Printed in the United States of America.

ISBN 0-940931-24-9

*To my wife, Linda
And our children, Julie, Laura, and Mary:
May Christianity flourish in their lifetimes.*

Books by John W. Robbins

Answer to Ayn Rand (1974)
The Case Against Indexation (1976)
The Case for Gold (Editor, 1982)
God's Hammer: The Bible and Its Critics (Editor, 1982, 1987)
Scripture Twisting in the Seminaries, Part 1: Feminism (1985)
Cornelius Van Til: The Man and the Myth (1986)
Education, Christianity and the State (Editor, 1987)
Pat Robertson: A Warning to America (1988)
War and Peace: A Christian Foreign Policy (1988)
The Pursuit of Power: Dominion Theology and the Reconstruction Movement (1988)

Contents

Foreword xi

Chapter 1 Who Is Pat Robertson? 1
               Robertson's Religious Experience 2
               The Robertson Network 3

Chapter 2 What Is Christianity? 6
               The Misuse of Language 7
               Christianity Defined 8
               A Revelation from God 9
               A Written Revelation 10
               The Limitations of Oral Revelations 11
               What Is the Gospel? 13
               Counterfeit Gospels 14
               Pat Robertson's Gospel 16
               The Gospel of Jesus Christ 18
               The Whole Counsel of God 19

Chapter 3 Hearing Voices 24
               Spurious Revelations 25
               Whose Voices? 29
               Testing the Prophets 31

Chapter 4 Doing Wonders 39
               The Miracles of Pat Robertson 40
               Satanic Miracles 44

　　　　　　　Divine Miracles 47
　　　　　　　The Dark Ages 49
　　　　　　　Positive Confession 50
　　　　　　　Extraordinary Divine Gifts Have Ceased 53

Chapter 5　**Twisting Scripture** 59
　　　　　　　Biblical Tongues 61
　　　　　　　Guidance 62
　　　　　　　The Sovereignty of God 68
　　　　　　　Predestination 73
　　　　　　　Salvation 74

Chapter 6　**Playing Politics** 76
　　　　　　　The Arrogance of Fanatics 77
　　　　　　　Robertson and Politics 79
　　　　　　　Robertson's Political Views 80
　　　　　　　Opposing Capitalism 83
　　　　　　　Foreign Policy 85
　　　　　　　The Bible and the Draft 88
　　　　　　　Foreign Aid 92
　　　　　　　Dominion Theology 93
　　　　　　　Public Education 94
　　　　　　　Conclusion 95

Chapter 7　**Beyond Reason** 96
　　　　　　　Mindless Religion 97
　　　　　　　Christ and Logic 98
　　　　　　　More Examples 101
　　　　　　　Irrationalism and the Demonic 103

Chapter 8　**President Robertson?** 106

Postscript:　**The Origin and Destiny of the
　　　　　　　Charismatic Movement** 109
　　　　　　　The Error of the Sects 109

      Wesleyanism 111
      American Revivalism and the Holiness Movement .. 112
      The Pentecostal Movement 115
      The Trend Toward Rome 116
      The Neo-Pentecostal or Charismatic Movement 117
      The Charismatic Movement and Rome 119
      A Fulfillment of Prophecy 120

Notes 122
Sources 132
Scripture Index 135
Index 139
The Crisis of Our Time 152
Intellectual Ammunition 159

Foreword

Pat Robertson, Republican candidate for President of the United States, is both very intelligent and very religious. He is a member of Phi Beta Kappa, the academic honorary fraternity, and a graduate of Yale Law School. He also claims to hear voices. He carries on conversations with the voices, he asks them questions, and the voices reply. Pat Robertson obeys the voices, which frequently command him to do certain things. He is fully convinced that the voices are the voice of God.

Pat Robertson is unique. No other major candidate for President in 1988, nor in any other year since the founding of the United States, has admitted to hearing and obeying voices. Even Abraham Lincoln, a deeply religious man tormented by a horrible and bloody war between brothers, a man who prayed daily for God's wisdom and guidance, never claimed to hear voices.

It is not Pat Robertson's claim to be a Christian that makes him unique. Many Presidential candidates, both successful and unsuccessful, have claimed to be Christians. Some of them undoubtedly were. But none of them has claimed to hear voices. Pat Robertson's claim is without precedent in the history of American politics.

Some people oppose Pat Robertson's candidacy because he professes to be a Christian. This writer does not agree with them. Their view is simply an example of secular bigotry against Christians. Being a Christian should not prevent one from running for and being elected to office. Some of the best men elected to office in the United States and in other countries have been Christians. What disqualifies a person for office is not his professed Christianity, but the belief that he hears voices. What is worse, Pat Robertson is convinced that the voices he hears ought to be obeyed.

The writer of this book is a Christian. He was raised in a Christian home in Pennsylvania. He attended two church-affiliated colleges before receiving an M.A. and a Ph.D. from The Johns Hopkins University. He attends a church which still believes that the Bible alone is the Word of God. He is the author of several books defending Christianity. His wife teaches in a Christian school—the same school their three daughters attend. And it is precisely because this writer is a Christian that he opposes Pat Robertson for President.

Christianity has been severely criticized and ridiculed in the past year as a result of Jim and Tammy Bakker's PTL scandals, the preposterous claims of Oral Roberts and other television fundraisers, and the candidacy of Pat Robertson for President. It is time that an effort be made to set the record straight: Neither the Bakkers, nor Oral Roberts, nor Pat Robertson represent Christianity. Neither their opinions nor their actions are taught in the Bible, and they are, in fact, hostile to Biblical Christianity. Their behavior should not be blamed on the Gospel of Jesus Christ.

In the pages that follow, Pat Robertson's astounding claims to perform divine miracles and hear the voice of God will be exposed as false. The reader will be provided with Robertson's own test to determine whether a prophet is false or true—and then furnished with the evidence of Robertson's failure of his own test. Robertson's interest in taking "dominion" over men and his messianic complex will be analyzed. And Christianity, which has suffered undeserved disrepute because of Robertson and his fellow Charismatics, will be distinguished from the Charismatic religion and defended against its detractors, both secular and religious.

If you are concerned about the future of our country, you ought to read this book.

If you are saddened and disgusted by the disrepute into which Christianity has fallen because of the statements and behavior of Charismatic preachers, you ought to read this book.

And if you are concerned about the future of Christianity, you *must* read this book.

Chapter One
Who Is Pat Robertson?

One may smile, and smile, and be a villain.
Hamlet, Prince of Denmark, I, 5.

The entry in the 1984-1985 edition of *Who's Who In America* occupies 21 lines:

ROBERTSON, MARION GORDON (PAT), clergyman, broadcast executive, writer, educator; born in Lexington, Virginia, March 22, 1930; son of A. Willis and Gladys (Churchill) Robertson; married Adelia (Dede) Elmer; children: Timothy, Elizabeth, Gordon, Ann. B.A., Washington and Lee University, 1950; J.D., Yale University, 1955; Master of Divinity, New York Theological Seminary, 1959; Doctor of Theology, honorary, Oral Roberts University, 1983. Ordained to the ministry of the Southern Baptist Church. Executive Assistant, W.R. Grace Company, 1954-1955; partner, Curry Sound Corporation, New York City, 1955-56; founder and president, Christian Broadcasting Network, Inc., Virginia Beach, Virginia, 1978—; member of the Presidential Task Force on Victims of Crime, Washington, 1982-83; Director, United Virginia Bank, Norfolk; and the National Religious Broadcasters, Morristown, New Jersey. Host: TV program *The 700 Club*, 1968—; author: *The Secret Kingdom*, 1982; *Shout It From The Housetops*, 1972; *My Prayer For You*, 1977. Served to First Lieutenant, United States Marine Corps, 1950-52. Recipient: Knesset medallion Israel Pilgrimage, International; Clergyman of the Year award, Religion in Media, 1981; Bronze Halo, Southern California Motion Picture Council, 1982; George Washington Honor medal, Freedoms Foundation at Valley Forge. 1983.[1]

Marion Gordon Robertson, son of attorney and United States Senator A. Willis Robertson, relative of two U.S. Presidents and a signer of the Declaration of Independence, is running for President.

Robertson's background lies in the gentry of southern Virginia. His father was Commonwealth Attorney for Rockbridge County, a member of the Virginia State Senate, a member of the U.S. House of Representatives for 14 years and a U.S. Senator for 20. His mother belonged to the same Churchill clan that produced Winston. Robertson is quite proud that his family tree includes a signer of the Declaration of Independence, Benjamin Harrison, and two Presidents of the United States, William Henry Harrison and Benjamin Harrison.

Marion Gordon Robertson was born March 22, 1930, in Lexington, Virginia, the younger of two sons. He entered Washington and Lee University in 1946, was elected to Phi Beta Kappa in his junior year, and graduated magna cum laude in 1950. Robertson studied "British culture" for a summer at the University of London in 1950. In 1948 he joined the Marine reserves, and he was called into active service on his return from England and shipped to Korea. After leaving the Marines he earned a law degree at Yale University Law School, "determined to be a lawyer and eventually a statesman like my father."[2] But he flunked the New York bar exam, derailing his political ambitions for thirty years. Hired by W.R. Grace company before he left Yale Law, Robertson was active in politics, chairing the 1956 Adlai Stevenson for President Campaign Committee on Staten Island, New York. He remained a Democrat until 1985.

Robertson's Religious Experience

After failing the New York State bar examination Robertson felt "God's calling" to become a minister. In April 1956 he "felt God's salvation in [his] life for the very first time. I could see [he wrote later] why evangelical Christians called the experience 'new birth.' "[3] His personal experience occurred during a dinner at a posh restaurant in New York City, a dinner to which he had been invited by a "handsome Dutchman" named Cornelius Vanderbreggen. Vanderbreggen's discussion centered on things religious, especially a "personal experience with Jesus Christ." What followed their conversation was "an indescribable sensation of joy and peace."[4]

Pat Robertson's 1956 religious experience convinced him that God was directing his life, and that he must do whatever God told him to do. His devotion to "God's call" is illustrated in this account of his early married life:

> The young mother had just entered the eighth month of a tiring pregnancy when her husband dropped a devastating piece of news. He felt a need, he said, to go to a rustic island in Canada [Campus in the Woods, Lake of Bays, Canada, operated by Intervarsity Christian Fellowship] for a few weeks to find communion with God. She would be left alone to manage her pregnancy, care for the couple's toddler son and supervise the family's move to a new house.
> Adelia (Dede) Robertson struggled mightily to change her husband's mind. She ridiculed him as a schizoid religious fanatic. She argued. She wept. She begged. But Marion G. (Pat) Robertson, then a budding seminarian, turned aside his wife's pleas with the unbending self-assurance that would later help him achieve remarkable success as a broadcaster and national religious leader. "This is God who's commanding me," he said.
> And so Robertson set off for his Canadian retreat, where he soon received an urgent letter from his wife: "Please come back. I need you desperately." [Robertson says, "I stood in my cabin for a long time, looking at the letter. Was this God telling me to go home, or was it Satan? I knew that this was no feminine ploy."[5]] The confused young husband called on God for advice and received clear guidance. He sat down and wrote his wife that she would have to get by without him.[6]

In 1958, after two years of desperate seeking, "tarrying," fasting, praying, and searching, "God blessed me [Robertson] with another kind of spiritual experience. His Spirit entered my life...."[7] This experience is central to understanding Robertson, for it is the focus of both his life and his books. He left his business career and entered New York Theological Seminary, from which he received a Master of Divinity degree in 1959. He was ordained a minister of the Southern Baptist Church in 1961, an ordination he retained until 1987 when he resigned to run for President.

The Robertson Network

In 1960 Robertson organized the Christian Broadcasting Network as a nonprofit corporation and bought a rundown UHF television station in Virginia's Tidewater region. Today CBN's annual revenues are estimated at $200-$240 million. The Christian Broadcasting Network and its related companies operate the fifth largest cable network in the country serving 34 million households containing 89 million people in 18,000 cities and towns. The companies also operate independent television stations in Dallas and Norfolk, Middle East Television in Lebanon, a domestic television network of 190 affiliate stations, a satellite radio network, a video cassette and book publishing division, a television and motion picture production division, offices and relief centers in 24 nations, and a crisis counseling division. Robertson's *700 Club* attracts an estimated 28 million viewers every month. And CBN is only part of the network.

Robertson is also Chancellor of CBN University, a graduate school with an enrollment of 944 that he founded in 1978; and he is the founder of the Freedom Council, another nonprofit, but political, organization established in 1981 and financed by CBN. In January 1986 the Freedom Council changed its name to the National Freedom Institute, and the same day a new Freedom Council was incorporated. The Institute was then dissolved in October 1986.

In 1982 Robertson was instrumental in forming the National Legal Foundation, a nonprofit organization. It was dissolved in 1985 and reincorporated the same day. It is financed by CBN and the Freedom Council. In 1985 Robertson organized the National Perspectives Institute, a research organization, and the Committee for Freedom, a multi-candidate political action committee (PAC). In 1986 he established his campaign committee, Americans For Robertson.

Robertson is also a member of the Executive Committee and a past president of the Council for National Policy, an exclusive organization of well-heeled conservatives.

According to *The New York Times*, "at least three tax-exempt organizations founded and directed by the Rev. Robertson, the television evangelist who is considering a bid for the Presidency, have given incomplete and false information to the Internal Revenue Service, according to interviews with former top officials of the organizations and an examination of public records."[8] As he enters the race for the Presidency in earnest, Robertson is also being hampered by a lawsuit that he filed against a former Member of Congress and Marine Veteran, Paul

McCloskey, who has charged that Robertson used his father's influence as a Member of Congress to keep himself out of combat duty in Korea.

In October 1987 *The Wall Street Journal* reported that Robertson had married his wife only ten weeks before the birth of their first child. At least he did not abandon her or force her to have an abortion. This, of course, occurred more than thirty years ago, before his religious experience in 1956. But Robertson, until the correct date was published in *The Wall Street Journal,* had been saying that he was married on March 22, 1954, rather than on August 27. In an interview with *The Washington Post* in July 1987, for example, Robertson said that he had been married on March 22, 1954.

Pat Robertson is also a bestselling author. His book, *The Secret Kingdom,* was the number one religious book in America in 1983. His most recent book, *America's Dates With Destiny,* had advance sales in hardback of 135,000 copies.

For more than thirty years Pat Robertson has been telling anyone who would listen, and he seems convinced himself, that God is commanding him to perform certain tasks. The commands are given by voices, sometimes still quiet voices, sometimes audible voices, level and conversational. Robertson has convinced many people that God does talk to him, and, consequently, when Pat Robertson talks, his followers listen. The question that faces America in 1988 is, Should a man who claims to hear and boasts of obeying voices be elected President of the United States? As a Christian this writer must answer, Certainly not. And we must begin the argument by explaining what Christianity is, and what it is not.

Chapter Two
What Is Christianity?

His divine power has given to us all things that pertain to life and godliness, through the knowledge of Him who called us.
2 Peter 1:3.

Pat Robertson claims to be a Christian, and he is not alone. Many Presidential candidates, past and present, have claimed to be Christians. Millions of individuals and thousands of organizations in the past two thousand years have claimed to be Christian. There are more than two thousand organizations in the United States alone in 1988 that profess to be Christian. Yet these organizations, let alone the particular individuals who compose them, differ dramatically.

Historically, for example, both the Roman Catholic church and the Puritans claimed to be Christians. Yet will anyone deny that Roman Catholicism, with its veneration of saints, its adoration of Mary, its use of images, beads, and statues, its clerical hierarchy, and its elaborate ritual and ostentatious costumes, is a different religion from iconoclastic Puritanism? Which one, then, is Christian?

Today the contrast is equally dramatic, if not so obvious as in the seventeenth century. There are small groups of people who still believe the religion of the Protestant Reformers and the Puritans; they believe that the Bible alone is the Word of God, that it is therefore without error; that Jesus Christ was an actual figure of human history, like George Washington or Abraham Lincoln; that He was God incarnate, born of the Virgin Mary; that He was crucified for the sins of His people, He rose again the third day and later ascended into Heaven, from where he will return to judge the living and the dead. They believe that Christ died to save only His people, and that He, being all-powerful, actually saved them from both sin and Hell. They believe that sinful men obtain right standing with God only on the basis of the imputed righteousness of Christ, not by anything they have done or can do, and not by anything God has done in their lives, nor by any experiences they may have had, but simply by the work Christ did on earth two thousand years ago.

In contrast to these few heirs of the Protestant Reformation, there is not only the 800 million member Roman Catholic church, there are also large Protestant churches that have repudiated the Reformation with its resounding affirmations of "The Bible alone" as the source of truth, "Faith alone" as the means of justification before God, "Grace alone," not human merit, as the reason for man's salvation, and "Christ alone" as the provider of that salvation. There are also groups such as the Mormon church, which claims to be Christian, the Unification church, which claims to be Christian, the Christian Scientists, and so on indefinitely. In the twentieth century there are thousands of differing groups that claim to be Christian. What then, in all this confusion, is Christianity? When a man like Pat Robertson says he is a Christian, what does he mean?

The Misuse of Language

Undoubtedly, Robertson would reply that he is a follower of Christ. After all, that is where the name "Christian" comes from: Christ. But such a reply is hardly helpful. Some people who say they follow Christ deny that He is the Second Person of the Trinity. Some even deny that He ever lived, or that we have any evidence that He ever lived. Others will admit that Christ lived, but deny that He rose from the dead. Yet they all claim to be followers of "Christ."

Religious confusion has progressed to such an extreme in this century that people who use the same words, such as "Jesus Christ," frequently are not talking about the same person or thing at all. In the early part of this century a Professor of New Testament at Princeton Theological Seminary observed that "the great redemptive religion which has always been known as Christianity is battling against a totally diverse type of religious belief, which is only the more destructive of the Christian faith because it makes use of traditional Christian terminology."[9]

This confusion began, in large part, because of insincerity and dishonesty. Men, especially the leaders in the churches at the end of the nineteenth and the beginning of the twentieth centuries, stopped believing the doctrines of the Bible. But rather than openly and honestly admitting that they no longer believed that the Bible was a revelation from God, and thereby losing their positions of influence, prestige, and pay, they concealed their unbelief by using the same words with new meanings. For example, it was common at one time for Christians to refer to the "divinity" of Christ. That meant that Jesus Christ was God as well as man. He was divine, and no mere man was. Jesus Christ was unique. But some clergymen who professed to be Christian started believing that every man is divine, simply because he is a man. Therefore, they could continue to say that they believed in the divinity of Christ, even while denying it. They no longer meant what the Bible teaches: that Christ is unique, that He alone is God incarnate. Yet they still affirmed that Christ was divine.

This confusion of meanings, which began in earnest about a century ago, has now reached the point that when a man says he is a Christian, the word is virtually meaningless. Even when he says that he believes in God or Christ, words which once were used as the Bible uses them, we are given little useful information. There are as many different notions of "God" and "Christ," it seems, as there are organizations calling themselves churches. Reincarnationists use the phrase "born again" to mean something quite different from what Christ meant in John 3. It takes a wise and a patient person to sort all the meanings out.

Christianity Defined

In order to avoid confusion this book will adopt a clear definition of Christianity. Rather than using words in an almost meaningless way—and they are meaningless precisely because they have been used to mean so many different things—we will define *Christianity* not as what people who call themselves Christians believe, or do, or feel, but as a body of teachings, as a book: The Bible. By *Christianity* we shall mean simply the statements in the sixty-six books of the Bible and all their logical implications. Christianity is best summarized in the *Westminster Confession of Faith*, which was written in London in 1648, and which at one time was the creed affirmed by all Presbyterian churches, and in slightly modified forms by Congregational and Baptist churches as well.

This is not a new way to approach this matter, although some readers may be surprised at such a definition of Christianity. This method of defining terms is used all the time in any field in which serious study and progress has been made. For example, should someone want to discuss Platonism, the ideas of the Greek philosopher Plato, he must first define *Platonism*. He does this by limiting it to the ideas found in the dialogues that Plato wrote. What Plato's students taught, and even less, what later philosophers said about him simply are not Platonism. Platonism is not what philosophers calling themselves Platonists think, but what Plato thought. If the same rules—or, more correctly, the same lack of rules—had been applied to the study of *Platonism* as have been applied to the study of *Christianity*, so that anything taught by anyone who called himself a Platonist automatically became Platonism, no progress in Platonic studies would have been possible. Unless terms are clearly defined, no progress can be made. The religious confusion and decadence of the twentieth century stems, in no small measure, from the lack of precise definitions.

A Revelation from God

Since we have clearly defined Christianity, we can proceed to make explicit some of its major doctrines. *The Westminster Confession of Faith* does this in thirty-three chapters. We can take only a fraction of that space here, but the reader is urged to study the *Confession* at length. Perhaps the best book to read on the subject is *What Do Presbyterians Believe?* by Gordon H. Clark. That book contains the full text of the *Confession*, and a very helpful commentary on it.

Christianity is, first of all, belief in the sixty-six books of the Bible as the Word of God. These books, this Bible, are, in the words of the first chapter of the *Westminster Confession*, "given by inspiration of God to be the rule of faith and life." Not *a* rule. Not one rule among several. *The* rule. The *only* rule. The authority of this book, as the book itself claims, does not depend on the testimony of any man or church, but wholly upon God, its author, who is truth itself. It is, therefore, to be believed because it is the Word of God. It is the authoritative book because it is the only book that is wholly true. And it is a true book because it was inspired—the word literally means "breathed out"—by God, who can neither lie nor make mistakes.

The Bible's claims to its own divine inspiration and truth run into the hundreds. Perhaps the most familiar is 2 Timothy 3:14-17, where Paul is writing his last instructions to his young friend and fellow teacher, Timothy:

> But as for you, continue in the things which you have learned and been assured of, knowing from whom you have learned them, and that from childhood you have known the Holy Scriptures, which are able to make you wise for salvation through faith which is in Christ Jesus. All Scripture is given by inspiration of God, and is profitable for doctrine, for reproof, for correction, for instruction in righteousness, that the man of God may be complete, thoroughly equipped for every good work.

There are many more similar verses: Second Peter 1:20-21 say: "No prophecy of Scripture is of any private interpretation [origin], for prophecy never came by the will of man, but holy men of God spoke as they were moved by the Holy Spirit." Jesus prayed for his disciples by saying: "Sanctify them by your truth. Your word is truth."[10]

When Christ responded to the temptation of the Devil, He always quoted Scripture: "It is written."[11] The reason is quite simple: Christ regarded the words of Scripture as the words of God. They were authoritative because they were true, and they were true because they had been revealed by God who is truth itself.[12]

A Written Revelation

This last reference makes a further point that we must understand. God not only has given men information that they could not otherwise know, but He has given it to them in a permanent form. The verses from 2 Timothy 3, for example, do not even mention the authors of Scripture; it is the written words of Scripture which are inspired. The Bible teaches that the words written by the human authors came from God. Now that the written revelation has been given, there is no more revelation as there was in times past: "God, who at various times and in different ways spoke in time past to the fathers by the prophets, has in these last days spoken to us by His Son, whom He has appointed heir of all things, through whom also He made the worlds."[13]

The apostle Peter made clear that he regarded the written word as a source of truth even more important than voices from Heaven. Here are his words:

> Moreover I will be careful to ensure that you always have a reminder of these things after my decease. For we did not follow cunningly devised fables when we made known to you the power and coming of our Lord Jesus Christ, but were eyewitnesses of His majesty. For He received from God the Father honor and glory when such a voice came to Him from the Excellent Glory: "This is my beloved Son, in whom I am well pleased." And we heard this voice which came from heaven when we were with Him on the holy mountain.
> We also have the prophetic word made more sure, which you do well to heed as a light that shines in a dark place, until the day dawns and the morning star rises in your hearts; knowing this first, that no prophecy of Scripture is of any private interpretation, for prophecy never came by the will of man, but holy men of God spoke as they were moved by the Holy Spirit.[14]

God gave a written revelation so that it would be a permanent revelation. The Bible is the "prophetic word made more sure," more sure than a voice from Heaven. Moreover, Peter commands us to study that written revelation until we understand it, "until the day dawns and the morning star rises in your hearts." We use the same figure of speech even today: When a person understands something, we sometimes say that it "dawned" on him.

The Westminster Confession summarizes the Bible's teaching about itself in these words:

> It pleased the Lord, at sundry times and in divers manners, to reveal himself . . . , and afterward, for the better preserving and propagating of the truth . . . to commit the same wholly unto writing; which makes the Holy Scripture to be most necessary, those former ways of God's revealing his will unto his people being now ceased.

The Limitations of Oral Revelations

If the reader played a game called "Gossip" as a child, a game in which a sentence is whispered into the ear of another player, and so on through several persons, and the sentence heard by the last player is finally compared to the sentence spoken by the first, he will have some idea what happens to ideas that are not written down. They simply are not preserved, not even for the few minutes it takes to play the game. Oral tradition is no substitute for writing. God's revelation was written down in order to preserve it. The prophets Isaiah, Jeremiah, Amos, and Moses, for example, all wrote down the words that God had spoken to them for our learning.[15]

But it was not simply for the preservation of the truth that God's entire revelation was written down, it was for the "better propagating" of it. If, in the game of Gossip, there are some players who want to distort the message for their own motives, no one can stop them. All that can be done is to compare the first sentence with the last. Now if you stretch that game out over centuries, making each player another generation, and the persons who started the oral tradition soon die, the men who pass on the oral tradition have total control over it. There is no first sentence by which to judge what the middle men call the oral tradition. Consequently, they can make the tradition say whatever they wish.

This is exactly what happened in the Dark Ages, when the Roman Catholic church tried to take control of Christ's teachings by preventing the common people from reading the Bible. The Roman clergy did not want anyone, especially uneducated laymen, to be able to compare what they were teaching with what the original revelation from God, the Bible, said. In 1229 the Roman Catholic Council of Valencia even placed the Bible on the *Index of Forbidden Books* with the following decree:

> We prohibit also the permitting of the laity to have the books of the Old and New Testament, unless any one should wish, from a feeling of devotion, to have a psalter or breviary for divine service, or the hours of the blessed Mary. But we strictly forbid them to have the above mentioned books in the vulgar [common] tongue.[16]

The Roman Catholic church's refusal to permit the common people to read the Bible in their own language was one of the causes of the Protestant Reformation. Roman Catholic church-states murdered men who had dared to translate the Bible into everyday language. One of the major tasks Martin Luther accomplished was the translation of the Bible into German.

The danger, or one of the dangers, of private revelations, whether they be called oral tradition or voices from God, is that they cannot be examined by others. God caused holy men to write His entire revelation down so that it would be open to inspection by all. This intention may be seen, for example, in the letters of the New Testament which are addressed to all Christians, not just to church leaders. In most of the letters, church leaders are not even mentioned. All Christians were to read, study, and believe the Bible. In that way, the distortion of the truth by those who claim to have private revelations or "oral tradition" may be eliminated.

The same point may be made in a political context by comparing written to unwritten constitutions. America's Founding Fathers wrote a Constitution so that every American would be able to know the limits of the federal government's power and thereby resist and correct its abuses of power. Unfortunately, the American people have largely forgotten what is in the Constitution (even as they celebrate its writing), just as they have largely forgotten what is in the Bible. The Constitution has virtually become a dead letter, and the courts, the Congress, the President, and the bureaucracies simply grasp as much political power as they can. A written revelation and Biblically literate Christians are indispensable to the purity, preservation, and propagation of Christianity, just as a written Constitution and a Constitutionally literate populace are indispensable to the survival of a free society. Christians are a people of The Book, not the Voice.

What Is the Gospel?

The confusion that plagues the religious world is not restricted to the meaning of the word *Christian*. The Gospel itself, which all who call themselves Christians should agree on, has become so confused by the opinions of men as to be almost meaningless. The ancient Tower of Babel has been replaced by radio and television towers as dozens of religious leaders teach their own gospels on the airwaves every day.

Pat Robertson, like many other American religious leaders, is called an "Evangelical." The word has its roots in the Greek New Testament, where the Gospel is called *euaggelion*, the good news. At the time of the Protestant Reformation in the sixteenth century, the word *Evangelical* was applied to the Reformers, for they believed and preached the good news, the Gospel, that Christ had earned salvation for His people, that men need not and could not earn salvation by their own works and experiences, and that this good news, this Gospel, was found in the Bible alone. The word *Evangelical* originally meant two things: (1) that the

Bible, not church leaders, nor clergymen, nor human experience, is the sole source of truth; and (2) that a sinner receives right standing before God by having Christ's righteousness reckoned to his account, through faith in the person and work of Christ. These ideas were expressed in two slogans: *sola scriptura*—Scripture alone—and *sola fide*—faith alone.

Today, however, there is a great deal of confusion about what the Gospel is, and what an Evangelical is, just as there is confusion about what a Christian is. Because of this confusion, many people are called Evangelicals who do not believe the Gospel. It might be best to begin to sort out this confusion by spelling out some of the popular religious ideas that are not the Gospel.

Counterfeit Gospels

The Gospel is not "You must be born again."
The Gospel is not "You must be filled with the Holy Spirit."
The Gospel is not "You must be baptized in the Holy Spirit."
The Gospel is not "You must speak in tongues."
The Gospel is not "You can perform miracles."
The Gospel is not "You must be saved."
The Gospel is not "Let Jesus into your heart."
The Gospel is not "You must have a personal relationship (or experience or encounter) with Christ."
The Gospel is not "Repent."
The Gospel is not "Expect a miracle."
The Gospel is not "Put Jesus on the throne of your life."
The Gospel is not "Jesus set an example for us so that we may follow Him to Heaven."
The Gospel is not "Trust Jesus."
The Gospel is not "Let go and let God."
The Gospel is not "Draw nigh unto God."
The Gospel is not "Christ died for all men and desires the salvation of all."
The Gospel is not "Decide for Christ."
The Gospel is not "Christians should take dominion over the earth."
The Gospel is not "Make Jesus Lord of your life."
The Gospel is not "Jesus is coming again."

All these messages, and presumably many more that I have neither heard nor thought of, are being preached from American pulpits and television studios as the Gospel. A few of them are commands taken from Scripture. But none of them is the Gospel. Not everything in the Bible is the Gospel. The Gospel is good news.

But the Gospel is good news of a particular sort. It is not good news about what Christians will enjoy in Heaven. It is not good news about what God can do in changing your life. It is not good news about the success, prosperity, health, money, and powerful living that God wants you to enjoy. Many people, like Pat Robertson, confuse the Gospel with stories about what God has done or can do in their lives. One looks in vain through Pat Robertson's books and newsletters for a presentation of the Gospel of Jesus Christ. What one finds instead are numerous accounts of miracles, speaking in tongues, and other amazing and exciting religious experiences. None of these things is the Gospel.

Robertson makes the same mistake that the seventy disciples did, as Luke reports in chapter 10. Let me repeat the story:

> After these things the Lord appointed seventy others also, and sent them two by two before His face into every city and place where He Himself was about to go . . . . Then the seventy returned with joy, saying, "Lord, even the demons are subject to us in your name."
> And He said to them, "I saw Satan fall like lightning from heaven. Behold, I give you the authority to trample on serpents and scorpions, and over all the power of the enemy, and nothing shall by any means hurt you. Nevertheless do not rejoice in this, that the spirits are subject to you, but rather rejoice because your names are written in heaven."

Unlike many religious people that falsely claim they can perform divine miracles, here were seventy men who could truly perform divine miracles. God was doing wonderful things in their lives. They had dominion even over demons. But Jesus tells them explicitly, "Do not rejoice in this." Christ gave them a direct and explicit command not to rejoice in their own experiences—experiences that some people today would promote as "power evangelism" and "power healing." The disciples were focusing on their own experience rather than what God had done from all eternity and what Christ was going to accomplish on the cross. They were rejoicing in their subjective experiences. But Christ told them to rejoice in something that they had never experienced, something that God had done wholly outside of them, even before they were born. He told them to rejoice in the doctrine of election—that their names are written in Heaven. That election is permanent: Their names are *written*. But many, if not all, of those who are promoting healing and miracles today actually deny the doctrine of election. They believe that man is free of God's control. Therefore, they have nothing to rejoice in but their own experiences.

Most of what are called "Evangelical" books, essays, television programs, and sermons consist of little more than stories about the wonderful things God is doing in this movie star's life, or that football player's life, or what He can do in your life. They do not contain even the least suggestion of the Gospel. It is impossible to overemphasize this point. Virtually all of what is preached from the pulpits and television studios of America, in conservative as well as in liberal churches, is not the Gospel. It is a clever counterfeit, and millions of churchgoers and television viewers are being cheated.

Pat Robertson's Gospel

Pat Robertson's gospel is a gospel of experience. He has had experiences that he wants to share with everyone. He has been "born again." He has been "baptized in the Spirit." He has spoken in "tongues." He has performed "miracles." He has heard the "voice of God" thousands of times. God has "nudged" him. God has given him "peace." One looks in vain through his books and newsletters for a discussion of the attributes of God, the origin of the Bible, the person and work of Jesus Christ—the historical Christ, not the experiential Christ—the definition of faith, or the meaning of justification. All the major doctrines of Christianity are either totally missing from his writings or mentioned in passing with little or no discussion.

Instead of the truth of the Bible and the Gospel of Jesus Christ, Robertson offers an entire book on how you too can perform miracles: *Beyond Reason;* two books about his life: *My Prayer For You* and *Shout It From The Housetops;* advice on how to manipulate God to get what you want: *The Secret Kingdom,* wherein the Laws of the Kingdom, which work for Christian and non-Christian alike, are spelled out in speculative detail; a superstitious account of American history, *America's Dates With Destiny;* and his *Answers to 200 of Life's Most Probing Questions,* most of which depend only slightly on the Bible.

In one of these books he tells people how to enter the "secret kingdom":

> Entrance into the Kingdom of God—the secret kingdom, the world of miracles, the miracle dimension—must be with knowledge of and submission to God's will and plan for you. In summary, I suggest these simple steps to enable you to experience the miraculous in your life:
> You must be spiritually reborn.
> **You must rely on the biblical mandate of authority.**
> You must be baptized in the Holy Spirit.
> You must be willing to persevere in faith.
> You must know how to pray.
> You must declare the will of God with authority.
> You must forgive if you have aught against anyone.[17]

About the only thing missing from this list of requirements for entrance into the Kingdom of God is believing the Gospel. It is not even mentioned.

In the Christmas 1980 issue of *The Flame,* Robertson informs us that he has a "social gospel": "I know that such a message would be criticized by many as being the 'social gospel.' Today, we have something more powerful than the message which John the Baptist brought. We have a Holy-Spirit-inspired, social gospel."[18] By this remark Robertson seems to mean that society and government, as well as individuals, ought to conform to God's moral standards. But his confusion of the requirements of the law with the Gospel, the good news, only makes clearer the fact that he does not preach the Gospel.

One of the things that strikes a reader of Robertson's books and newsletters is his constant emphasis on experience. Phrases and words such as, "felt," "sensed," "experience," "impression," "a feeling of excitement," "feel guided," "leading," "guiding," "waves of liquid love," and "a river of peace washing over me" are almost too numerous to count. They appear hundreds of times in his writings. The vocabulary of experientialism and the self-centeredness of his religion are unmistakable. This is precisely the attitude that Christ rebuked in the passage quoted above. None of these things has anything to do with the Gospel.

The Gospel of Jesus Christ

In contrast to Robertson's near total reliance on his subjective religious experience, the apostle Paul tells us what the Gospel is in 1 Corinthians 15:

> Moreover, brethren, I declare to you the Gospel which I preached to you, which also you received and in which you stand, by which also you are saved, if you hold fast that word which I preached to you—unless you believed in vain.
>
> For I delivered to you first of all that which I also received: that Christ died for our sins according to the Scriptures, and that He was buried, and that He rose again the third day according to the Scriptures.

That is the Gospel, and that Gospel is preached in very few so-called Christian churches today: Christ died for our sins according to the Scriptures, He was buried, and He rose again the third day according to the Scriptures.

Because of contemporary religious confusion, there are several aspects of Paul's Gospel that demand elucidation. First, the Gospel concerns history, not legend or myth. It is not, as Peter says, "cunningly devised fables."[19] When Paul mentions Jesus Christ, he means an actual historical character like George Washington or Julius Caesar. He is not speaking of an experiential "Christ" whom we imagine. There are many different "Christs" and "Gods" being talked about today.‡ The words *Jesus, Christ,* and *God* have become almost meaningless in the twentieth century, as we have seen, and unless one says exactly which "Christ" he means, no one, including himself, can know. Paul does that. His Christ is an historical figure, not a voice, nor a vision, nor a dream.

Second, the Gospel concerns the past, neither the present nor the future. It is history. The Gospel does not describe any present or future action that God or man might take. The Gospel is news about actions God in Christ took 2000 years ago to save His people, actions that are wholly outside of our experience. Just as all men are condemned by Adam's sin,‡‡ which was wholly outside of us, so are all of God's chosen

---

‡ The Biblical Christ predicted this when He said, "Take heed that no one deceives you. For many will come in My name, saying, 'I am the Christ,' and will deceive many" (Matthew 24:4-5).

‡‡ Romans 5:12, 18: "Therefore, just as through one man sin entered the world, and death

What Is Christianity? / 19

people saved by Christ's obedience unto death, which is wholly outside of their experience.‡‡‡ Just as the Gospel is history, not legend; and just as the Gospel concerns the past, not the present nor the future; so the Gospel is about something that God did, not something that we must do or can do. Christ is both the author and the finisher of our salvation.[20] We do not complete what He began; Christ said, "It is finished."[21]

Third, the Gospel concerns what Christ did for *His* people: Christ died for *our* sins, not for the sins of everyone in the world, but for the sins of His people only. He did not die for the sins of Judas, for example, for Judas went to Hell.[22] If Christ had died for Judas's sins, why was Judas sent to Hell? Was it for his unbelief, his failure to "let Jesus into his heart"? But unbelief and failure to "accept" Christ admittedly are sins, and Christ, according to this false but popular gospel, died for all of Judas's sins. So the question remains unanswered: If Christ died for all men, why are some men punished in Hell?[23]

The Scriptures teach that Christ did not die for all men.[24] He came to Earth to save some men, whom the Bible calls "His people,"[25] "the sheep,"[26] "friends,"[27] and "the church,"[28] among other names, and He actually earned salvation for them. He did not come merely to offer salvation to all men and hope that some men would accept His offer. He came to save His people, and He did so.

The Gospel is an objective and historical message. It does not concern our experiences at all. It does not concern our works, but God's works. It does not concern our alleged miracles, but Christ's death and resurrection. Regeneration—sometimes called the new birth, sanctification, faith, and the Second Coming are all consequences of what Christ accomplished 2000 years ago in Judea. They must not be confused with the Gospel, for effects should not be confused with causes.

The Whole Counsel of God

But there is more in Paul's account of the Gospel than might appear in a superficial reading. What we have discovered so far is totally different from what passes for the Gospel in this decadent age. But there

---

through sin, and thus death spread to all men, because all sinned . . . . Through one man's offense judgment came to all men, resulting in condemnation."

‡‡‡ Romans 12:10: "For if when we were enemies we were reconciled to God through the death of His Son, much more, having been reconciled, we shall be saved by His life."

is a great deal more. Paul uses the phrase "according to the Scriptures" twice in this concise account of the Gospel. His whole summary of the Gospel takes only twenty-seven words in the *New King James* translation (and fewer in the Greek), and eight of those words are "according to the Scriptures, according to the Scriptures." The phrase is obviously very important. Why does Paul repeat it? What does it mean?

The Gospel, according to Paul, is embedded in something much larger: It is embedded in all the Scriptures. Not only are the Scriptures the only reliable source of information we have about the life, death, burial, and resurrection of Christ, but the Scriptures alone explain those events. The Gospel is not merely that Christ died; so did Paul. The Gospel is not merely that He was buried; so was Abraham. The Gospel is not merely that Christ rose again. So did Lazarus. The Gospel is that Christ died for our sins according to the Scriptures. And that He rose again the third day according to the Scriptures. The Gospel is in accord with and explained by the Scriptures, all sixty-six books of them. When Christ explained His resurrection to the disciples He did so by explaining the Scriptures:

> And beginning at Moses and all the Prophets, He expounded to them in all the Scriptures the things concerning Himself . . . .
> Then their eyes were opened and they knew Him; and He vanished from their sight. And they said to one another, "Did not our heart burn within us while He talked with us on the road, and while he opened the Scriptures to us? . . ."
> And He opened their understanding, that they might comprehend the Scriptures.[29]

By emphasizing the phrase "according to the Scriptures," Paul is emphasizing the fact that the Gospel is part of a system of truth given to us in the Bible. All of the parts of this system fit together. All the statements in the Bible are logically consistent with one another.[30] To give but one example of this, Christ's birth, life, death, and resurrection fulfilled specific prophecies given centuries earlier. The exact town where He would be born was predicted hundreds of years before His birth;[31] the fact that His birth would be unusual, for His mother would be a virgin, was predicted centuries before His birth;[32] His death among the wicked and His burial among the rich were predicted;[33] and Christ himself predicted His resurrection.[34] The specific propositions that Paul calls the Gospel in 1 Corinthians 15 do not stand alone. They imply and are implied by many others. The choosing by God the Father of those that should be saved, the suffering of the punishment due them for their sins by Jesus Christ at Calvary, and the gift of faith to the elect people by God the Holy Spirit are all part of the system of truth taught in the Bible. They are the three great aspects of redemption: election, atonement, and faith. And the Gospel, the doctrine of the atonement, is the central theme. It is impossible to defend the Gospel, or even to preach the Gospel, without defending and explaining the system of truth of which it is a part.

Paul's emphatic phrases in 1 Corinthians 15 indicate that those who wish to separate the Gospel from the system of truth found in the Bible cannot do so. The Gospel, while a distinct *part* of the Biblical system, is nevertheless a part of the *system*. This system is fully expressed in the Scriptures. The propositions that Paul calls the Gospel are some of the propositions of Scripture. Because the Gospel is part of the Scriptural system of truth, it is impossible to defend the Gospel without defending the whole system. An exclusive emphasis on the "fundamentals" of the faith, rather than the "whole counsel of God," which is the phrase the Bible uses,[35] is futile. Six or eight unconnected truths, even if they be major doctrines of Christianity, are not the whole of Christianity, and cannot be defended effectively. Fundamentalism poses no serious threat to secular philosophies, because it is logically unsystematic and disjointed, a mere shadow of the robust Christianity we find in the Bible.

Paul emphasized the Scriptures, but this emphasis upon the writings is not unique to Paul. When explaining and defending Christianity, Christ always appealed to Scripture, and never to His own experience. During His temptation in the wilderness, Christ quoted Scripture in reply to each of the Devil's temptations: "It is written," "It is written," "It is written." What makes this appeal more significant is the context in which it occurred. Christ had just been baptized in the River Jordan by John the Baptist. He had heard a voice from heaven saying, "This is My beloved Son in Whom I am well-pleased." The Holy Spirit had descended on Him in the form of a dove. Talk about religious experiences! No one else, before or since, has ever had such an astonishing experience. Yet Christ did not tell the Devil what had happened to Him, the voice from heaven and the giving of the Holy Spirit. Why not? Why did Christ ignore all this and quote what many today call the dead letter of the Bible? Why does Christ answer the Devil by quoting Scripture rather than recounting His recent and unique spiritual experiences? Because the Scriptures are the objective written Word of God. The Bible, not our experiences, is authoritative. If Christ did not appeal to His experience, and it was a far greater experience than any mere man could ever hope to have, there is absolutely no justification for our appealing to our miserable and possibly deceptive experiences.

It was, in fact, the Devil who wanted Christ to appeal to His personal experiences: He wanted Christ to perform a miracle; Christ refused. He wanted Christ to take a leap of faith off the pinnacle of the temple, presuming God the Father would perform a miracle; Christ refused. He wanted Christ to worship him, avoid the hellish suffering of the cross, and thereby gain dominion over all the kingdoms of the world; again Christ refused.[36]

The Devil used the same appeal to experience in the Garden when he tempted Eve: He promised Eve that she would become godlike when she ate the forbidden fruit. And Eve "saw that the tree was good for food, that it was pleasant to the eyes, and a tree desirable to make one wise."[37] Relying upon her experience, and seeking a still more wonderful experience, Eve abandoned the Word of God. The secret of Christ's intransigent resistance to diabolical temptation was precisely the fact that He did not prefer His own experiences to the Word of God.

The apostle Peter also emphasizes the written Word of God. He climaxes his account of the testimony concerning the truth of the Christian faith by mentioning Scripture. In his second letter Peter says,

> For we did not follow cunningly devised fables when we made known to you the power and coming of our Lord Jesus Christ, but were eyewitnesses of His majesty. For He received from God the Father honor and glory when such a voice came to Him from the Excellent Glory: "This is My beloved Son, in Whom I am well pleased." And we heard this voice which came from heaven when we were with Him on the holy mountain.
>
> We also have the prophetic word made more sure, which you do well to heed as a light that shines in a dark place, until the day dawns and the morning star rises in your hearts.[38]

A few verses earlier Peter had written that God's "divine power has given to us all things that pertain to life and godliness, through the knowledge of him who called us."[39] Please notice the phrase "all things." Later in the same chapter Peter again says that Scripture is the *only* way we have of getting this knowledge: Scripture, the prophetic word made more sure, is the light that shines in a dark place.[40] Not a brightly lit place, nor even a dimly lit place, but a dark place. There is no other source for this knowledge, including knowledge of the Gospel, than the Scriptures. The Bible claims to have a monopoly on truth. The Charismatics, like all other cults and false religions, deny that monopoly. They denigrate the Bible and base their religion on their personal experiences.

But the Gospel is neither accounts of our personal experiences nor commands that we are to obey. The Gospel is the good news of what Christ did for His people 2000 years ago. It is not about the new birth, nor the Second Coming, nor the activities of the Holy Spirit in our hearts. The Gospel is propositions about historical events that happened wholly outside of us. It has consequences and implications for us today, to be sure, but these consequences are *effects* of the Gospel, and must not be confused with the Gospel itself. The fatal error of the Dark Ages was to confuse God's work for us with God's work in us, and so pervert the Gospel. The same error is widespread among so-called Evangelicals today who do not distinguish between what Christ has done for us and what the Holy Spirit can do in us. We are rapidly re-entering the Dark Ages because the light and clarity of the Gospel have been lost.

Now that we have established who Pat Robertson is, what Christianity is, and what the Gospel is, let us turn to a closer examination of Mr. Robertson's theological opinions and how they affect his political ambitions.

Chapter Three
Hearing Voices

Thus says the Lord of hosts: "Do not listen to the words of the prophets who prophesy to you. . . . They speak a vision of their own heart, not from the mouth of the Lord. . . . The prophets prophesy lies in My name. I have not sent them, commanded them, nor spoken to them; they prophesy to you a false vision. . . . Every word of God is pure; He is a shield to those who put their trust in Him. Do not add to His words, lest He reprove you, and you be found a liar.
Jeremiah 23:16; 14:14;
Proverbs 30:5-6

The Bible makes some extraordinary claims for itself. For example, 2 Timothy 3:16 and 17 say:

All Scripture is given by inspiration of God, and is profitable for doctrine, for reproof, for correction, for instruction in righteousness, that the man of God may be complete, thoroughly equipped for every good work.

If you are a student of the Bible, you have probably read these verses before, but perhaps you have not completely understood what they mean. Notice the universal words, the words that make no exceptions: *All, complete, thoroughly,* and *every.* God says that the entire Bible is profitable for teaching, for correction, for rebuking, and for training in righteousness. Not just part of it, but all of it—*all* Scripture. It was *all* God-breathed—that is what *inspiration* means—and it is therefore all true.

Because it is all true it is all profitable. In fact, the Bible is so profitable, nothing else is needed.

The Bible claims that it is sufficient to make the man of God *complete*, to equip him *thoroughly* for *every* good work. The Bible does not equip a man of God for some good works but not for others. Nor does it partially equip a man of God for all good works. The Bible equips a man of God *completely* for *every* good work. Not only does the Bible claim to be true, it claims to be complete. Nothing else is needed. It is both the necessary and the sufficient source of truth. The Bible claims to have a monopoly on truth. That is why the *Westminster Confession of Faith* makes this statement:

> The whole counsel of God, concerning all things necessary for his own glory, man's salvation, faith and life, is either expressly set down in Scripture, or by good and necessary consequence may be deduced from Scripture: unto which nothing at any time is to be added, whether by new revelations of the Spirit or traditions of men.[41]

The *Confession* piles up universals just as the Bible does: *whole, all, nothing, any.* It accurately reflects the emphatic statements of Scripture.

If the Bible's claim is true, then the claims of the Charismatic movement, the Roman Catholic church, the Mormon church, the Christian Science church, the Muslim religion, the Unification church, and many other religions to have direct revelations and oral messages from God are false. God has given men of God all the information they need in the Bible. It is only men who are not of God who desire such additional "revelations."

Spurious "Revelations"

One of the distinctive marks of a cult is its reliance on revelation from sources other than the Bible. Here is what one of the foremost authorities on cults says:

> (1) *An Extra-Scriptural Source of Authority*.... Since, in distinction from non-Christian religions, they [cults] claim to be Christian groups, they must somehow appeal to the authority of the Bible. Yet in order to justify their peculiar doctrines they must either correct Scripture, reinter-

pret Scripture, or add other sources of authority to Scripture. Their attitude toward Scripture is therefore always an ambivalent one: a mixture of apparent subjection to its authority and of arbitrary manipulation of its teachings.... The Bible itself condemns the attempt to supplement it with any additional source of authority.... The claim of the cults to have a source of revelation beyond the Scriptures... is a claim which places them outside the pale of Christian churches.[42]

It is, then, very unfortunate that men who believe that they receive messages directly from God have been elevated by way of television to the position of speaking for Christians in the political arena. But it is also unfortunate—and a clear and present political danger—that a man who believes these things is running for President. What Pat Robertson believes and teaches simply are not Christian ideas. His claims to direct revelations from God are astonishing for their sheer audacity. But because he wears a three piece suit and a Phi Beta Kappa key, because he is a graduate of Yale University Law School and the son of a U.S. Senator, because he has built a multi-million dollar broadcasting network, people tend to ignore, or believe, the extraordinary and supernatural claims he makes for himself. Here are just a few of them:

> In my unending quest for wisdom, it turned out that the "word of wisdom" was a miracle of God that developed special meaning for me. All the gifts of the Spirit are exceedingly important when springing from faith, hope, and love; but the supernatural bestowal of the word of wisdom is to be cherished.
> The word of wisdom ... is a glimpse into the future regarding a specific event or truth. It is an unveiling ....
> I was praying one day in 1969, and the Lord spoke plainly to my inner man: "The stock market is going to crash."
> This was startling, for I hadn't even been thinking about the stock market. Then He added, "Only the securities of your government will be safe ...."
> That revelation has, I believe, application in the present [1982], when a worldwide financial collapse seems imminent ....
> And the Lord has steadily increased this miraculous manifestation in my life ...."[43]

***

Probably the most frequent occurrence of the miraculous in my life has involved the word of knowledge, touching on physical or emotional healing or other interventions by the Lord in the lives of people.[44]

Over the years I have personally experienced thousands of such words of knowledge . . . .[45]

***

When my meal of cantaloupe and cottage cheese arrived, I bowed my head to say grace—and the Lord began to speak to me about the site [for the Christian Broadcasting Network] three thousand miles away . . . .

"I want you to buy the land," the Lord said. "Buy it *all*," He said. "I want you to build a school there for My glory, as well as the headquarters building you need."[46]

***

To be filled with the Spirit of God and to be led and instructed by God's Spirit should be a normal part of a Christian's life. God normally speaks to our inner being in a still, quiet way. However, there are times when He speaks in a audible voice.[47]

I was praying and fasting some years ago, seeking to understand God's purpose more fully. I heard His voice, level and conversational, "What do I desire for man?"

A bit surprised, I replied, "I don't know, Lord. You know."

"Look at Genesis, and you'll see," He said.[48]

God had spoken to me. I had learned to know His voice.[49]

***

"I'm Pat Robertson . . . . God has sent me here to buy your television station . . . . God's figure is $37,000, and the station has to be free from all debts and encumbrances . . . . I'm not going to give you anything for it [an option to buy], but God wants the option now."[50]

***

"How much can you spend?" he [the representative of RCA] asked.

I waited. Then the Lord spoke, "Don't go over $2½ million."

"Ed," I said, "our top limit is $2½ million."[51]

Some readers may have forgotten that Jim and Tammy Bakker got their start in religious television with Pat Robertson. He hired them in 1965 to host a puppet show for children. The Bakkers had been traveling "evangelists" for the Assemblies of God denomination. It was Jim Bakker who put Robertson's "first big telethon" over the top. With one hour to go, and $40,000 short, Bakker started crying on the air, and the telephones lit up like Christmas trees. Robertson not only got the $40,000 he wanted, but a good deal more. In fact, it was Jim Bakker, not Pat Robertson, who started the *700 Club* program, against Robertson's better judgment.[52] Bakker stayed with Robertson for several years before he and Tammy turned their tear ducts into rivers of money for their own show, the *PTL Club*.

Once when he was still with Robertson, Bakker became a little rebellious, refusing to go on the air when ordered to do so by the station manager. Here is Robertson's account of the episode:

> Jim Bakker had been an invaluable worker.... I loved Jim like a brother, but knew that I had to uphold discipline or the whole station would become an anarchy....
>
> The next morning, after I finished my radio program, "Powertime," I started out of the studio when I heard the voice of God: "Don't fire Jim Bakker...."
>
> Thursday morning I was sitting at my desk when Jim Bakker walked back into the station.... [H]is eyes were red from weeping. "God has really been dealing with me," he said. "I don't think I should leave. I feel that God wants me here. I've never been more miserable in all my life, and I want to come back."
>
> "Well, I'm delighted to have you back, but we still have to do something about this fine," I said. [Robertson had fined Bakker $100 for insubordination, and Bakker had quit.]
>
> I had levied the fine, and the staff expected me to make it stick; yet God had told me not to fire Jim (even if he didn't pay the fine). So I finally gave the $100 to Jim, and he paid the fine, to the satisfaction of the staff.[53]

God, according to Robertson, gives him investment advice—does this make Robertson guilty of insider trading?—tells him which land and equipment to buy and what prices to pay for them, endorses U.S. Treasury bills and bonds, informs him what will happen in the future, instructs him to eat breakfast, directs him which Bible verse to look up, commands him not to fire Jim Bakker, and reveals to him what is going on in the minds and lives of other people. Moreover, Robertson tells us that this is normal: "To be led and instructed by God's Spirit should be a normal part of a Christian's life." But Robertson's religion is neither Christian nor normal.

Whose Voices?

There are difficulties with these "revelations," and Robertson mentions a few himself. First there is the difficulty of distinguishing God's voice from the Devil's:

> There is no way of knowing for certain that someone is hearing from God, unless that person has been listening to God over a long period of time and then testing what he or she has heard. Such people have become accustomed to discerning God's voice. There are many others, however, who think they are hearing from God when maybe they are not.[54]
>
> There is no shortcut to spiritual understanding. You have to learn to walk with God and to know His voice; otherwise, you will mistake your own voice for His. You even may be fooled by the voice of Satan, or you may hear the clamoring voice of the world. It is so easy to get these voices mixed up.[55]

Then there is the problem of sin:

> The thing that clouds our view is sin. But once the sin is forgiven, we are to enter boldly into the throne room of grace and commune with God by the Spirit, who communicates with our spirit. It's a bit like tuning into a radio or television station. You get on the right frequency and you pick up a program. So it is with listening to the Lord. He is speaking constantly, but we are often on the wrong frequency.[56]

Being on the wrong frequency can also cause us to get the wrong message. Robertson himself has gotten the wrong message from his voices at times. For example, he got the call letters for his television station wrong, choosing WTFC rather than WYAH. "Now I was forced to go back to my supporters," he wrote, "and tell them I had erred and run ahead of God's plan. It looked bad, because once you admit a mistake in the area of guidance, it indicates you are prone to make others. I had already made several."[57]

Another example of Robertson's mistakes in hearing the voice of God appears in a chapter revealingly entitled "An Angel of Light" in his autobiography, *Shout It From The Housetops*. He tells a story about being fooled by a woman who claimed to be an illegitimate daughter of H.L. Hunt, the Texas billionaire. The chapter title is revealing because it refers to 2 Corinthians 11:13-15, which read:

> For such [people who boast of being men of God] are false apostles, deceitful workers, transforming themselves into apostles of Christ. And no wonder! For Satan himself transforms himself into an angel of light. Therefore it is no great thing if his ministers also transform themselves into ministers of righteousness, whose end will be according to their works.

This woman's story involved an enormous deception, which cost CBN thousands of dollars, but which, while it was occurring, had all the appearances of being a message and gift from God. Colleagues came to Robertson with dreams and reports of hearing the "voice of God" in the bathroom prophesying a large financial gift to CBN; there were unusual coincidences which Robertson took as confirmations from God that this was indeed God's will; and Robertson himself fasted and prayed and "sensed peace about the entire matter."[58] But he was dead wrong.

In the 1950s Robertson had visited the gravesite of the heretical nineteenth century revivalist Charles Finney:

> It was as though we were on holy ground, and we kicked off our shoes and began laughing and praising God. I knew the Holy Spirit had allowed us to come to this place for a sign. He was about to pour himself out on us even as he did on Finney.
> Even though we did not receive the baptism in the Holy Spirit that weekend as we hoped . . . .[59]

But it was not a mere hope that was disappointed. Robertson said that "I knew the Holy Spirit had allowed us to come to this place for a sign. he was about to pour Himself out on us." Again Robertson was dead wrong about his "signs."

On yet another occasion he reported his worship experience this way:

> Our initiation came in the form of Spirit-led worship. We would wait on God, and then he would give a psalm, a hymn, a prophecy, a portion of Scripture. On one occasion as we were praying, Dick White felt led to read a particular Psalm. While he was reading, the number of a hymn flashed in my mind. I was totally unfamiliar with the Presbyterian Hymnbook, but I picked it up and opened it to the page number that had come to my mind. There before my eyes was that particular Psalm set to music.
>
> Such experiences in worship caused me to realize that God could lead me directly through the Scriptures and personal revelation. I recognized it as training for whatever ministry the Holy Spirit was preparing for me, even though I had no idea what that ministry was to be. All I knew was that it was to be the kind of ministy where I would often have to rely on just such revelations, and that this time was to be used in purifying myself so the percentage of error would grow less. To rely on this kind of direct guidance for your life's course, and not to have a clear channel, could lead to immediate disaster.[60]

Robertson was into "channeling," it seems, long before it became popular in southern California.

Later on his wife was to warn: "Before now, Pat, when you got the wrong hymn from a hymnbook because someone had given a wrong prophecy, no great harm was done. But when you begin getting figures about how much to pay for a television station, then you can get in big trouble—not that we're not already in trouble."[61] Robertson's "percentage of error" is apparently quite high. Is this the man—is this the sort of man—who ought to be President?

Testing the Prophets

How can one tell what the correct message is and whether the voice one hears is the voice of God, or of Satan, or of the world, or one's own imagination? Robertson seems to think that practice makes perfect. His goal was to reduce the "percentage of error" in such revelations, for error could lead to disaster.

In one of the quotations above, Robertson mentions testing. At another point he tells us briefly what this testing consists of: "The Bible says that we can tell if someone is a prophet by seeing if what he has said comes to pass. That is a very pragmatic test, and it works."[62] The verse that Robertson is referring to, according to his note, is Deuteronomy 18:22. The relevant passage reads as follows:

> But the prophet who presumes to speak a word in My name, which I have not commanded him to speak, or who speaks in the name of other gods, that prophet shall die.
> And if you say in your heart, "How shall we know the word which the Lord has not spoken?"—
> When a prophet speaks in the name of the Lord, if the thing does not happen or come to pass, that is the thing which the Lord has not spoken; the prophet has spoken it presumptuously; you shall not be afraid of him.

Now this passage does not say what Robertson thinks it says. He asserts that "we can tell if someone is a prophet by seeing if what he has said comes to pass." But the Bible says that we can tell if someone is a *false* prophet by seeing whether his predictions fail to come to pass. The Bible does not say that we can determine who is a prophet from God by seeing whether his predictions come to pass. In fact, just a few chapters earlier in Deuteronomy 13, God says that he will cause false prophets, who will perform genuine miracles and make prophecies that are later fulfilled, to appear in Israel in order to test the people:

> If there arises among you a prophet or a dreamer of dreams, and he gives you a sign or a wonder, and the sign or the wonder comes to pass, of which he spoke to you, saying, "Let us go after other gods which you have not known, and let us serve them," you shall not listen to the words of that prophet or dreamer of dreams, for the Lord your God is testing you to know whether you love the Lord your God with all your heart and with all your soul. You shall walk after the Lord your God and fear Him, and keep His commandments and obey His voice, and you shall serve Him and hold fast to Him.
> But that prophet or that dreamer of dreams shall be put to death, because he has spoken in order to turn you away from the Lord your God, who brought you out of the land of Egypt and redeemed you from the house of bondage, to entice you from the way in which the Lord your God commanded you to walk. So you shall put away the evil from your midst.[63]

This passage from Deuteronomy unequivocally declares that some false prophets will perform miracles and make accurate predictions. Robertson's misunderstanding and misrepresentation of what the Bible says about testing prophets is an elementary logical blunder. When the Bible says that an unfulfilled prophecy betrays a false prophet, it does not imply, for it logically does not follow, that a fulfilled prophecy reveals a true prophet. A false prophet may prophesy falsely or truly, but a true prophet must prophesy truly. Because a false prophet may prophesy truly, one cannot conclude from the fulfillment of prophecy that a prophet is from God. False prophets would have little credibility if everything they said were false. It is only because they mix their falsehoods with truth, or with the appearance of truth, that they are able to persuade some people.

The logical blunder Robertson makes has a name: denying the antecedent: If p (false prophecy), then q (a false prophet) does not imply if not p (true prophecy), then not q (a true prophet). Robertson could have easily avoided this blunder if he had read Deuteronomy 13, where we are explicitly told that God will send false prophets whose prophecies will be fulfilled, and who will perform signs and wonders in order to test the people, to see if they will remain faithful to the written revelation that God had already given them. This Biblical teaching that false prophets can make accurate predictions and perform signs and wonders utterly destroys Robertson's position. He wants to be known as a true prophet because his predictions come true, and he can perform miracles. But false prophets can do and have done the same. Therefore, no number of fulfilled prophecies and miracles can establish Robertson or anyone else as a prophet or man of God, but a single unfulfilled prophecy can establish that he is a false prophet.[64]

Let us illustrate how the test works. David Wilkerson, one of Robertson's friends and a fellow Charismatic, prophesied in 1972: "I prophesy that within the next twelve months the Berlin Wall is coming down and there is going to be free access to all Iron Curtain countries including Russia."[65] The prophecy failed. The Berlin Wall remains, even in 1988. It has been reinforced since 1972 and made more dangerous. Access to Communist countries is still restricted. It follows necessarily that Wilkerson is, therefore, a false prophet. If Robertson also fails this test, he will be neither the first nor the last Charismatic to be revealed as a false prophet.

Since Robertson has indicated by his own words that he believes this manner of testing those who claim to be prophets is still in force, and since he claims to be a prophet, if not the Messiah himself,‡ he must also

---

‡ At the end of *Shout It From The Housetops*, Robertson blasphemously quotes Luke 4:18

be judged by his own words. Let us, then, look at a few of his own predictions that have not come true.

In the November/December 1978 issue of *Pat Robertson's Perspective*, Robertson wrote: "The rampaging inflation, credit squeeze, stock market plunge, dollar collapse, and skyrocketing price of gold which command headlines this fall were easily predictable in 1977 and early 1978."[66] If that were the case, one wonders why Robertson wrote as late as March 1978 that "It is still too early to read the economy this year."[67] Apparently Robertson's prophetic abilities failed him here.

In November 1979 Robertson wrote in his newsletter, *Pat Robertson's Perspective,*

> At present the odds are about 85-15 that we will experience a major world-wide depression in the early 1980s. From study of the 50-year Jubilee of the Old Testament, I had research done to determine if major depressions followed the biblical pattern. We learned that major depressions occurred in the United States every 56 years....
>
> Subsequent reading indicated that a Russian economist, N.D. Kondratieff, who wrote in the 1920s, had also posited a long-wave economic cycle of 54 years in Western economies. Kondratieff observed the phenomenon, but lacking biblical background, was unable to explain why it happened ....
>
> Fifty years after 1929 is 1979. If the cycle is 54 years, the next major depression is due in 1983. If the cycle is 56 years, the date would be 1985. If the standard is only 50 years, then we can expect a major collapse anytime between now and 1985."[68]

Although there was a recession in the early 1980s, there was no major world-wide depression. But the depression, insisted Robertson, began in 1982:

> In 1982 the economy of the world has reached the point where further growth of the nature that we have known since 1945 is virtually impossible. A contraction (depression) is beginning.... The fall of 1982

---

and 19, verses which apply to Jesus Christ, and seems to apply them to himself: "The Spirit of the Lord is upon me, because he has anointed me to preach the gospel to the poor; he hath sent me to heal the brokenhearted, to preach deliverance to the captives, and recovering of sight to the blind, to set at liberty them that are bruised, to preach the acceptable year of the Lord."

will see a time of panic or near panic in the financial markets . . . .
In the April 1980 Perspective I wrote these words which are being fulfilled in 1982:
King Louis XIV of France said, "Apres moi, le deluge."
The deluge will come between 1980 and 1984.[69]

The deluge did not come betwen 1982 and 1984. As a matter of fact, the longest period of economic expansion in the United States since World War II began in 1982. The Dow-Jones averages more than doubled between 1982 and October 1987, when the stock market crashed—an event unpredicted by Robertson.

The major 1982 depression, a principal theme in his newsletters, would be followed by a Soviet attack on the Middle East and a nuclear war "on an awesome scale." "This future war," Robertson predicted, "will see the Soviet military machine annihilated when God intervenes on behalf of Israel and her new allies . . . . Probably by 1982, when vast U.S. fiscal deficits have brought on a severe economic depression, the Soviets will launch a major aggression in the Middle East."[70] If there was an "awesome" nuclear war in the early 1980s, or a depression, this writer missed them. He hopes his readers did as well.

In the January 1980 issue of *The Flame*, we find these words:

> I believe that Jesus has given me a clear word, and I want to share it with you . . . .
> Within five years there will undoubtedly be a currency collapse and world depression of alarming proportions. During the same period, Russia will probably invade the Middle East and strike at Israel, causing a major war. On top of that, some astronomers forecast unusual gravitational pull on our planet when all of the planets line up in 1981—the so-called "Jupiter effect . . . ."
> In short, we will soon be entering turbulent days, and what is done in Jesus' name must be done quickly.[71]

In December 1979 Robertson wrote:

> Almost certainly there is going to be a major economic depression in the world. Almost certainly by 1982 the powerful Russian colossus will move in the Middle East and we will find ourselves locked in a struggle for survival.[72]

In February 1982 Robertson predicted that

Sometime this fall we should expect a clear and dramatic move by the Soviets to extend their grip on the Middle East.

The onrush of events toward the end of the year may see the world in flames. Remember that these events are clearly foretold by the prophet Ezekiel.[73]

The February/March 1980 issue of *Pat Robertson's Perspective* is entitled, "Special Issue: Prophetic Insights for the 'Decade of Destiny.' " It is filled with several pages of "prophetic insights" that have failed to occur as predicted.

In the fall of 1980 Robertson predicted, "we can expect a major Soviet thrust within two years, and lesser military actions prior to that time."[74]

After the Israeli invasion of Lebanon in 1982, Robertson predicted that "Israel has set off a slow burning fuse which will not be extinguished until the Middle East and possibly the world is in flames." A Soviet-led invasion of Israel, "during which Israel will be exalted and Russia destroyed, is very near—possibly as near as the fall of this year."[75]

On May 20, 1982, Robertson said:

> The Bible says that . . . the Soviet Union is going to make a move against this little nation known as Israel. And that's got to happen because it is very clear cut in the Bible in the last days; and along with the Soviet Union there is going to be Iran, there is going to be Ethiopia, possibly Libya, some East German forces which are now in South Yemen, this is going to happen . . . . [T]here is going to be a move by the Soviet Union into the Middle East.[76]

In 1985 *The Wall Street Journal* reported that "He [Robertson] says he no longer believes—as he once told his followers—that the Bible predicts a nuclear war and the beginning of the end of the world in the 1980s."[77] But Robertson cannot get off that easily. He claimed to be giving "prophetic insights," "clear words from Jesus," and "prophecies." If one of them is wrong, and the list we have compiled contains far more than one, then Robertson is not who he claims to be—*by his own test.*

One major prediction, made not by Robertson, but about Robertson by his friend and director of CBN, Harald Bredesen, is that Robertson will usher in the Second Coming of Christ. Here is how Robertson puts it:

It was May 1968.... Harald Bredesen stood behind me and began to speak. I knew I was hearing the voice of the Lord through Harald... "The days of your beginning seem small in your eyes in light of where I have taken you, but, yea, this day shall seem small in light of where I am going to take you, ... for I have chosen you to usher in the coming of My Son."

I have cherished those words for the past 12 years. I saw the fulfillment of the first part of that prophecy in 1979 as we dedicated the new CBN Center.... Without question, God had fulfilled His word.

But what of the second part of that prophecy? "... for I have chosen you to usher in the coming of My Son." We have not seen that as yet. However, God's people around the world are beginning to sense the awesome realization that historical events are fulfilling Bible prophecy at an ever-increasing pace...

Nearly two thousand years ago, John the Baptist was chosen by God to prepare the world for the coming of Jesus.... Much like John, CBN stands today in television's vast wasteland and cries out to the world, "Repent, ye: for the kingdom of heaven is at hand." We, too, have been chosen to prepare the way for the Lord. And Jesus is coming again, soon.[78]

The March 1979 issue of *The Flame* praises Robertson for the accuracy of his prophecies in these words: "Pat's warnings for the future are based on evidence drawn from the Bible. His visions are revealed by the Lord and are astoundingly accurate."[79]

What is astounding is that such blatantly false assertions can be made and believed by thousands of people. Leaving aside for the moment Robertson's high opinion of himself, what must we conclude from all these failed predictions? Do they reveal Pat Robertson as a false prophet? They certainly do. He has failed the Biblical test that he himself has recommended. But even if all Robertson's predictions had proven correct, he would still be a false prophet, simply because his doctrine is not Biblical doctrine. He has departed from the revelation that God has given in the Bible. He fails the test that all false prophets fail, even though they may be capable of performing signs and wonders: He teaches falsehoods. Moreover, he claims to be receiving revelations from God after revelation has ceased. The penalty for making such claims is a severe one:

> For I testify to everyone who hears the words of the prophecy of this book: if anyone adds to these things, God will add to him the plagues that

are written in this book; and if anyone takes away from the words of the book of this prophecy, God shall take away his part from the Book of Life, from the holy city, and from the things which are written in this book.[80]

That warning against adding to and taking away from the completed revelation from God appears in the last chapter of the last book of the Bible. All those who claim to speak for God, to get messages from God, or to hear God's voice, are condemned by God Himself writing in Scripture. They await God's judgment.

Chapter Four
Doing Wonders

An evil and adulterous generation seeks after a sign.
                                                    Matthew 12:39.

    We all have experiences, but only some of us believe that experiences, hunches, impressions, feelings, ideas, and notions are messages from God. This writer is having an extraordinary experience even as he writes these lines: I am watching little characters dance across a computer screen. Only a minuscule portion of the earth's population has ever seen such a thing. But is it a message from God? Hardly.

    When this writer worked as chief of staff for a Member of Congress, it was one of his duties to make sure the mail was answered properly and promptly. Some people like to write to public figures, especially Congressmen, and tell them their troubles. One correspondent from New York was convinced that the letters and numbers on license plates were messages intended for him. For example, the license plate WGY 885 meant: We'll get you in August 1985. This fellow was absolutely certain that someone in the New York State Department of Motor Vehicles was sending him threatening messages through license plates.

    Many people would regard this particular New York State resident as crazy and urge that he be confined to a rubber room. He was, however, a megalomaniac. He thought himself so important that the government of New York was going to extraordinary lengths to send him messages via their license plates. The man was sinfully conceited.

The Miracles of Pat Robertson

Had the egomaniac from New York been of a more religious bent, he could have concealed his conceit more easily, and collected millions as well, by claiming to get messages from God and performing "miracles." Pat Robertson is not only convinced he gets messages from God, he is convinced that he performs miracles as well—miracles just like those performed by God Himself, Jesus Christ. He has written an entire book extolling some of the alleged miracles he has seen and performed, and here are a few of the paragraphs from it and his other books:

> The age of miracles is not past. In fact, many believe that we are standing on the threshold of a visitation from God upon our world of such power that seemingly incredible miracles will then seem commonplace ....
> ... [T]hese true-life stories from our twentieth century are just a tiny part of the millions of miracles that are taking place in the lives of ordinary people around the world today.[81]

It should be pointed out that Christ Himself did not perform millions of miracles. In fact, in the entire Bible, spanning several thousand years of human history, there are fewer than one hundred miracles recorded. Moses and Joshua performed about 25; Elijah and Elisha performed another 25; and Christ and the apostles performed about 50. It seems counterproductive for miracles to be performed by the millions, as Robertson claims. After all, miracles derive their power from being unusual events, not commonplace. A multitude of miracles is self-defeating. When everything is a miracle, nothing is.

> Since I entered into a serious, intimate relationship with God through a commitment to Jesus Christ back in 1956, I have encountered tens of thousands of miracles....[82]
> I personally know of hundreds of people whose cancer was diagnosed as terminal but who have been miraculously healed.[83]

Kathryn Kuhlman, the late faith healer whom Robertson fondly quotes in his books, made similar claims to have witnessed many miracles. Dr. William Nolen, a Christian physician, investigated Kuhlman's claims and reported the results in his book, *Healing: A Doctor in Search of a Miracle*. Dr. Nolen describes a Kathryn Kuhlman healing service:

> Finally it was over. There were still long lines of people waiting to get onto the stage and claim their cures, but at five o'clock, with a hymn and final blessing, the show ended. Miss Kuhlman left the stage and the audience left the auditorium.
>
> Before going back to talk to Miss Kuhlman I spent a few minutes watching the wheelchair patient leave. All the desperately ill patients who had been in wheelchairs were still in wheelchairs. In fact, the man with the kidney cancer in his spine and hip, the man whom I had helped to the auditorium and who had his borrowed wheelchair brought to the stage and shown to the audience when he had claimed a cure, was now back in the wheelchair. His "cure," even if only a hysterical one, had been extremely short-lived.[84]

Like Robertson, Kuhlman wrote a book about miracles; hers was entitled *I Believe in Miracles*. In the book she tells of the many cancer victims she had cured, or rather, that God had cured through her. In an effort to find a miracle, Dr. Nolen wrote to Kuhlman for a list of the cancer patients who had miraculously recovered.

> I wrote to all the cancer victims on her list—eight in all—and the only one who offered cooperation was a man who claimed he had been cured of prostatic cancer by Miss Kuhlman. He sent me a complete report of his case. Prostatic cancer is frequently very responsive to hormone therapy; if it spreads, it is also often highly responsive to radiation therapy. This man had had extensive treatment with surgery, radiation, and hormones. He had also been "treated" by Kathryn Kuhlman. He chose to attribute his cure —or remission, as the case may be—to Miss Kuhlman. But anyone who read his report, layman or doctor, would see immediately that it is impossible to tell which kind of treatment had actually done most to prolong his life.[85]

Kathryn Kuhlman suggested the names of eighty-two other people who had been cured of various diseases. Dr. Nolen studied twenty-three of those cases as well—only twenty-three wished to cooperate—and concluded that not one of the so-called healings was legitimate.[86] But let us continue with Pat Robertson:

Each year through my *700 Club* television program, I see or hear about some fifty thousand people who have received miraculous answers to prayer—most of them instantaneous. Tumors and cysts disappear, cancer is healed, disfiguring scars vanish, twisted limbs straighten, retarded children develop mental acuity, diseased organs become normal, marriages are restored, miracles of finance take place.[87]

Prayer is the link between finite man and the infinite purposes of God. In its ultimate sense, it consists of determining God's will and then doing it on earth . . . .

If we fully believe God and have discerned His will, Christ said that we may translate that will from the invisible world to the visible by the spoken word. In short, God uses the spoken word to translate spiritual energy—sheer power—into the material.

The most vivid illustration, of course, was the creation of the world. God spoke to the void and said, "Let there be light," and there was light. . . .

In like manner, our partnership with God is fulfilled when we speak His word in the power of the Holy Spirit . . . . Have faith in God, know who He is, know what He is doing, trust His favor upon us, participate with Him. What we say in His name should then come to pass.[88]

Once He has spoken to us, we are to speak after Him. If we do, miracles occur.[89]

We must see that, by living in the kingdom now, we enter back into what man lost in the Garden of Eden. We return to the authority God gave us at the Creation . . . .

Through our words, we translate the will of God in the invisible kingdom to the visible situation that confronts us. We speak to money, and it comes. We speak to storms, and they cease. We speak to crops, and they flourish.[90]

Because of the desperate condition of our world, we still need miracles today. That means we need to understand the law [of miracles] and act on it, for Jesus introduced a new order of normality at the Day of Pentecost. With the power of the Holy Spirit, miracles were to be normal. He expected His followers to do even greater things than He did.[91]

Jesus Christ performed miracles. The Apostles Peter and Paul performed miracles. Other of the disciples performed miracles. And *you* can perform miracles if you but understand the power of God and the laws of faith and obedience that unlock God's power to those who believe in Him and serve Him.[92]

Without in any way advocating fanaticism, I believe God would enable man, under His sovereignty, to deal successfully with the conditions that threaten the world with catastrophic earthquakes.... I am convinced that were man to turn from his wicked ways and seek the Lord, he would be able to take dominion over the faults in the earth's structure and render them harmless.... Similarly, man, taking his rightful place under God, would subdue the causes of drought and famine. World hunger would cease.[93]

God's prerogative to manage the elements also comes across clearly in this series of questions posed by Agur, son of Jakeh, in Proverbs 30:4: "Who has gone up to heaven and come down? Who has gathered up the wind in the hollow of his hands? Who has wrapped up the waters in his cloak? Who has established all the ends of the earth? What is his name, and the name of his son? Tell me if you know!"

The answer to these questions, of course, is "God." Yet there are times, especially in dire emergencies, when humans who have a deep relationship with God can exercise extraordinary power over the land, the seas, and the weather.[94]

Robertson claims to have performed two miracles of turning hurricanes away from the Virginia coast. The following account concerns the first, Hurricane Betsy, in 1978:

> Word reached us that a great killer hurricane with winds exceeding 150 miles per hour was heading directly into our area.... Our resources were so limited then that, short of a miracle, we would have had a hard time recovering from such a disaster.
>
> I immediately knew that our only sure shield of protection was prayer. So I began to talk to God about that hurricane. I described my view of the problem we faced, and I asked for his help. But nothing happened. No answer came to me....
>
> The next morning, I attended a meeting of the local chapter of a Christian fellowship group [Full Gospel Businessmen's Fellowship International].... At about 10:30 A.M., I was called upon by the chairman to pray....
>
> As I prayed out loud in that meeting, faith rose within me, and with authority in my voice, I found myself speaking to a giant, killer hurricane about one hundred miles away in the Atlantic Ocean.
>
> Specifically I commanded that storm, in the name of Jesus, to stop its forward movement and to head back where it had come from.... Even as I write these words, I know it may seem absurd to talk to a giant hurricane. But that was what the Holy Spirit led me to do, and that's exactly what I did.

After I left the prayer meeting at noon that Saturday, I turned on my car radio. A bulletin on the national news reported that the forward progress of Hurricane Betsy had been stopped at 10:30 A.M. that morning —the precise time when a little group of Christians had ordered it to do so.[95]

Make no mistake about it: Robertson is claiming that he can perform miracles—miracles of healing, miracles of nature, financial miracles—just as Christ Himself did. He even once—at least he admits to doing it once—tried to raise a child from the dead, like Christ. After witnessing a traffic accident in which a little girl was injured, Robertson recalls,

Then we told him [the surgeon caring for the girl], "We are asking God for a miracle. It's going to happen. Please keep working with her . . . ."

Then we really began to pray. We spoke divine healing over the unconscious child. We anointed her with oil. We rebuked the death angel and forbade him to take her. We called upon the Lord with all the faith we could muster.

About six o'clock that evening, the child died. But we weren't finished. We continued to pray. The mortician came and took away her body. After he had embalmed it, he placed her in an open casket in the church on Monday evening.

We refused to accept what had happened and went into the church to pray that the child would rise from the dead.

She did not rise and we buried her on Tuesday.[96]

This failed "miracle" is another example of Robertson'a failure to pass the test for prophets. He predicted a miracle that did not happen: "We are asking God for a miracle. It's going to happen." The false prophets of ancient Egypt failed to duplicate all of Moses's miracles.[97] Had Moses failed to perform as he said he would, he would have been no better than they.

Satanic Miracles

It is not the contention of this author that the age of miracles is past. Neither Robertson's failure to raise the little girl from the dead nor Nolen's failure to find a genuine cure among the victims of Kathryn

Kuhlman proves that the age of miracles is past. It most assuredly is not. Miracles have been performed in many centuries, including the twentieth. But that, of course, does not mean that the miracles are from God. The Devil can perform miracles as well. Many verses in Scripture teach this; here are a few of them:

> If there arises among you a prophet or a dreamer of dreams, and he gives you a sign or a wonder, and the sign or the wonder comes to pass, of which he spoke to you, saying, "Let us go after other gods which you have not known, and let us serve them," you shall not listen to the words of that prophet or that dreamer of dreams, for the Lord your God is testing you . . . . But that prophet or that dreamer of dreams shall be put to death . . . .[98]

This passage explicitly says that God caused false prophets and miracle workers to appear among the ancient Israelites in order to test His people. False prophets may appear today for the same reason: "For false christs and false prophets will arise and show great signs and wonders, so as to deceive, if possible, even the elect."[99] This verse, as well as some of those that follow, teach that God causes false prophets and miracle workers to appear in order to deceive those whom He has not chosen to be saved.

> Not everyone who says to Me, "Lord, Lord," shall enter the kingdom of heaven, but he who does the will of My Father in heaven. Many will say to Me in that day, "Lord, Lord, have we not prophesied in Your name, cast out demons in Your name, and done many wonders in Your name?" And then I will declare to them, "I never knew you; depart from Me, you who practice lawlessness!"[100]
>
> The coming of the lawless one is according to the working of Satan, with all power, signs, and lying wonders, and with all unrighteous deception among those who perish, because they did not receive the love of the truth, that they might be saved.[101]
>
> Then I saw another beast coming up out of the earth, and he had two horns like a lamb and spoke like a dragon. And he exercises all the authority of the first beast in his presence, and causes the earth and those who dwell in it to worship the first beast, whose deadly wound was healed. He performs great signs so that he even makes fire come down from heaven on the earth in the sight of men. And he deceives those who dwell

on the earth by those signs which he was granted to do in the sight of the beast.... [102]

And I saw three unclean spirits like frogs coming out of the mouth of the dragon, out of the mouth of the beast, and out of the mouth of the false prophet. For they are spirits of demons, performing signs, which go out to the kings of the earth and of the whole world.... [103]

Then the beast was captured, and with him the false prophet who worked signs in his presence, by which he deceived those who received the mark of the beast.... [104]

The evidence from Scripture that Satan and his ministers can perform miracles is abundant and overwhelming. Therefore, the performance of miracles does not establish anyone as a spokesman for God. He may very well be a spokesman for the Devil. Christ certainly gave many warnings about false prophets, false teachers, and false christs who would try to deceive even the elect. God uses such false prophets not only to test His people, but finally to deceive some of those whom He has condemned to Hell.

In the first chapter of Galatians the apostle Paul sounds the clearest possible warning against such false teachers and prophets:

> I marvel that you are turning away so soon from Him who called you in the grace of Christ, to a different gospel, which is not another; but there are some who trouble you and want to pervert the gospel of Christ. But even if we, or an angel from heaven, preach any other gospel to you than what we have preached to you, let him be accursed. As we have said before, so now I say again, if anyone preaches any other gospel to you than what you have received, let him be accursed.[105]

Since the Devil and his ministers can perform miracles, the ability to perform miracles does not necessarily distinguish true prophets from false. The final test of a prophet, or of an angel, or of an ordinary preacher, the test that separates the true from the false, is, What does he teach? Moses in Deuteronomy 13 states the doctinal test; Isaiah repeats it;‡ Christ in Matthew emphasizes it; and Paul in Galatians makes it

---

‡ Isaiah 8:19-20: "And when they say to you, 'Seek those who are mediums and wizards, who whisper and mutter,' should not a people seek their God? Should they seek the dead on behalf of the living? To the law and to the testimony! If they do not speak according to this word, it is because there is no light in them."

unmistakably clear. The test is not, Does he perform miracles? Even the Devil and his ministers can perform miracles:

> For such are false apostles, deceitful workers, transforming themselves into apostles of Christ. And no wonder! For Satan himself transforms himself into an angel of light. Therefore it is no great thing if his ministers also transform themselves into ministers of righteousness, whose end will be according to their works.[106]

It follows that Pat Robertson's claim to have witnessed or performed thousands of miracles is worthless either in establishing his claim to be a prophet or in getting him into Heaven.

Divine Miracles

To determine whether there are any divine miracles occurring today, as opposed to Satanic miracles, which seem to be plentiful, one must determine God's purpose in performing miracles. That purpose was to attest to the divine mission of his messengers. When Moses brought a message from God to the Israelites and to Pharaoh, he could perform miracles. So with Elijah and Elisha, and Jesus and the apostles. But not all prophets performed miracles: John the Baptist, the greatest of the prophets before Christ, did not.[107]

If the only purpose of divine miracles is to attest to the divine origin of God's messengers, it follows that when God's revelation is complete, no further miracles are to be expected. This is exactly what we observe in church history. Of course the cessation of divine miracles does not prove that their purpose was to attest divine messengers. That purpose may be discerned in Exodus 4:1-5:

> Then Moses answered [God] and said, "But suppose they will not believe me or listen to my voice; suppose they say, 'The Lord has not appeared to you.'"
> So the Lord said to him, "What is that in you hand?"
> And he said, "A rod."
> And He said, "Cast it on the ground." So he cast it on the ground, and it became a serpent; and Moses fled from it. Then the Lord said to Moses, "Reach out your hand and take it by the tail" (and he reached out his hand and caught it, and it became a rod in his hand), "that they may believe that

the Lord God of their fathers, the God of Abraham, the God of Isaac, and the God of Jacob, has appeared to you."

The purpose of miracles may also be understood from Acts 2:22: "Men of Israel, hear these words: Jesus of Nazareth, a Man attested by God to you by miracles, wonders, and signs which God did through Him in your midst, as you yourselves also know . . . ."

Since the purpose of divine miracles is to attest divine messengers, miracles were last performed during the age of Christ and the apostles, the last of the divine messengers, that is, during the first century A.D. Miracles are, in fact, called the "signs of an apostle":

> Then fear came upon every soul, and many wonders and signs were done through the apostles.[108]
> And through the hands of the apostles many signs and wonders were done among the people.[109]
> Truly the signs of an apostle were accomplished among you with all perseverance, in signs and wonders and mighty deeds.[110]

With the deaths of the apostles, and of the men on whom they had laid their hands, thus transferring to them the power of performing miracles, the miracles ceased. The men on whom the apostles laid their hands could not, in turn, transfer the gift of giving the power of working miracles to anyone else. That is why Simon the sorcerer sought out the apostles: He realized that if he wanted to obtain the ability to give the power to perform miracles, he had to get it from the apostles themselves, for only they had that ability: "Now when Simon saw that through the laying on of the apostles' hands the Holy Spirit was given, he offered them money, saying, 'Give me this power also, that anyone on whom I lay hands may receive the Holy Spirit.' "[111] Had this power, which belonged to the apostles alone, been obtainable from ordinary Christians blessed by the apostles, Simon's action would be inexplicable.

In the first 50 years of the second century A.D., there is little or no evidence of divine miracles. Even during the lifetimes of the apostles one can see the gradual disappearance of divine miracles. Prominent in the Gospels and in the early chapters of the book of Acts, divine miracles gradually decrease, until there is virtually no mention of apostolic miracles in the epistles. In fact, there are cases of illness mentioned in

Paul's letters, such as Timothy's problem with his stomach, that Paul does not heal. He simply recommends that Timothy drink a little wine rather than water to help his stomach.[112] As the apostles finish their divine task of writing Scripture, writing down all that Christ had commanded them to write, the miracles waned. The written word made the signs and wonders superfluous. When Scripture was complete, oral revelation and divine miracles ceased.

The Dark Ages

But demonic miracles, long present in heathen religions, infiltrated the decadent church during the Middle or Dark Ages. Beginning in the fourth century, two hundred years after the death of the last apostle, the accounts of miracles begin to increase in a crescendo reaching the present day. One scholar has written, "Every religious possession the heathen had, indeed, the Christians, it may be said broadly, transferred to themselves and made their own."[113] The cult of the saints emerged in the Dark Ages, and with it the cult of relics. Not only could the saints perform miracles, but their possessions, parts of their bodies, indeed anything that had contacted them in any way, could allegedly perform miracles as well.

> Christians seem to have been inspired rather with eagerness to reap the fullest possible benefit from their saints; and, reasoning that when a body is filled with supernatural power, every part of the body partakes of this power, they broke the bodies up into fragments and distributed them far and wide. The insatiable lust to secure such valuable possessions begot in those who trafficked in them a callous rapacity which traded on the ignorance and superstition of the purchasers. The world was filled with false relics, of which, however, this is to be said—that they worked as well as the true . . . .
>
> The absurdity is equally great, however, when we hear of the Christians preserving feathers dropped from the wings of Gabriel when he came to announce to Mary the birth of Jesus; and . . . when we read of pilgrim monks boasting of having seen at Jerusalem the finger of the Holy Spirit. Any ordinary sense of the ridiculous, however, should be sufficiently satisfied by the solemn exhibition in the church of Saints Cosmas and Damien at Rome of a "vial of milk of the Blessed Virgin Mary." . . . [T]his is far from the only specimen of Mary's milk which is to be seen in the

churches. Several churches in Rome have specimens, and many in France . . . and Spain . . . .[114]

Robertson himself recognizes the absurdity of some of these preposterous claims, even while he defends the use of "prayer cloths":

> There is certainly nothing improper about prayer cloths. It is possible to bless a piece of cloth or paper, send it to somebody else and, on account of the prayer attached to it, see healing take place. That type of miracle has happened in the past and happens today.
> However, this also can be a device for charlatans, who sell magic amulets and such. In the Middle Ages, mountebanks sold objects of veneration such as milk from the Virgin Mary and splinters from the true cross. They reportedly sold enough splinters from the true cross to build a church!
> This sort of thing still goes on.[115]

Indeed it does, and sending of prayer cloths to the superstitious and ignorant people who watch religious television programs is one example of it. Robertson has no reason to scoff at the counterfeit miracles of the Dark Ages and the Roman Catholic church as long as he defends "miraculous" prayer cloths. Miracles are the stock in trade of every false religion, Roman, Greek, Babylonian, Egyptian, and Persian. There is a shrine in Constantinople dedicated to Our Lady of Lourdes, one of the principal miracle-shrines of the Roman Catholic church. It is "a place of pilgrimage and a source of miraculous cures" for Christians, Jews, and Muslims.[116]

Positive Confession

One of the miracle-working practices that Robertson recommends is positive confession. He claims that this is a method for performing miracles used by God the Father and Christ the Son. Robertson writes, "Confess His abundance in your finances and you will see it. Confess His healing in your relationships and harmony will appear. Confess his protection over your life and you will walk in safety."[117]

> Right now, in this life, He would have us stop cajoling and begging.‡
> He would have us live in the kingdom, in harmony with Him, receiving His

---

‡ God's desire on this point, however, does not seem to apply to fundraising telethons.

> thoughts by the Spirit. As the Apostle Paul said, ". . . We have the mind of Christ." So speak that mind, Jesus was saying in the fig tree episode. Speak his thoughts.[118]
>
> Solomon wrote: "From the fruit of a man's mouth he enjoys good . . . ." In other words, when you confess blessing, favor, victory, and success, those things will come to you.[119]
>
> I am convinced that if a person is *continuously* in sickness, poverty, or other physical and mental straits, then he is missing the truths of the kingdom . . . . He has missed the prosperity I believe the Scripture promises.[120]

What does this statement about sickness, poverty, and suffering imply about the apostle Paul or John the Baptist, for example? God told Ananias about Paul: "For I will show him how many things he must suffer for My name's sake."[121] Paul prayed repeatedly that his "thorn in the flesh" be removed, but it was not:

> And lest I should be exalted above measure by the abundance of the revelations, a thorn in the flesh was given to me, a messenger of Satan to buffet me, lest I be exalted above measure. Concerning this thing I pleaded with the Lord three times that it might depart from me. And He said, "My grace is sufficient for you, for My strength is made perfect in weakness." . . . Therefore, I take pleasure in infirmities, in reproaches, in needs, in persecutions, in distresses, for Christ's sake. For when I am weak, then I am strong.[122]

At another time Paul wrote:

> Are they ministers of Christ?—I speak as a fool—I am more: in labors more abundant, in stripes above measure, in prisons more frequently, in deaths often. From the Jews five times I received forty stripes minus one. Three times I was beaten with rods; once I was stoned; three times I was shipwrecked; a night and a day I have been in the deep; in journeys often, in perils of waters, in perils of robbers, in perils of my own countrymen, in perils of the Gentiles, in perils in the city, in perils in the wilderness, in perils in the sea, in perils among false brethren; in weariness and toil, in sleeplessness often, in hunger and thirst, in fastings often, in cold and nakedness . . . .[123]

Paul's argument in these verses is that his claims to be a minister of

Christ are substantiated by his sufferings for the sake of the Gospel. Others, who claimed to be ministers, had no such evidence. Shall we say with Robertson that the apostle Paul "missed the truths of the Kingdom?" Or that John the Baptist, who lived in the wilderness eating locusts and honey, "missed the prosperity that Scripture promises"? Or shall we say with Christ, "Remember the word that I said to you, 'A servant is not greater than his master.' If they persecuted Me, they will also persecute you."[124] Or shall we say with Pat Robertson, "We speak to money, and it comes. We speak to storms, and they cease. We speak to crops, and they flourish"?[125]

Positive confession is a growing movement among certain cults and New Age groups. Dave Hunt[126] has capsulized its teachings, all of which are found in Robertson's books:

1. **Faith is a force that both God and man can use.**

Jesus Christ performed miracles. The Apostles Peter and Paul performed miracles. Other of the disciples performed miracles. And *you* can perform miracles if you but understand the power of God and the laws of faith and obedience that unlock God's power to those who believe in Him and serve Him.[127]

2. **Faith's force is released by speaking words.**

If we fully believe God and have discerned His will, Christ said that we may translate that will from the invisible world to the visible by the spoken word. In short, God uses the spoken word to translate spiritual energy—sheer power—into the material.

The most vivid illustration, of course, was the creation of the world. God spoke to the void and said, "Let there be light." and there was light. . . .

In like manner, our partnership with God is fulfilled when we speak his word in the power of the Holy Spirit . . . . Have faith in God, know who He is, know what He is doing, trust His favor upon us, participate with Him. What we say in his name should then come to pass.[128]

3. **Man is a little God in God's class.**

We must see that, by living in the kingdom now, we enter back into what man lost in the Garden of Eden. We return to the authority God gave us at the Creation . . . .

Through our words, we translate the will of God in the invisible kingdom to the visible situation that confronts us. We speak to money, and it comes. We speak to storms, and they cease. We speak to crops, and they flourish.[129]

The answer to these questions [of who controls the weather], of course, is "God." Yet there are times, especially in dire emergencies, when humans who have a deep relationship with God can exercise extraordinary power over the land, the seas, and the weather.[130]

4. Anyone can use the faith force or the laws of the kingdom.

Jesus quite bluntly said, "If you do this, then this will happen." When he added no restrictions as to time, place, nationality, and the like, then they were laws, in the same sense as the natural laws established by God—those governing motion, gravity, sound and such. They simply work.[131]

These are not just Christian and Jewish principles, any more than the law of gravity is Christian and Jewish. We are talking about universal laws. The laws of gravity, thermodynamics, and electromagnetism work for everybody.[132]

5. You get what you confess.

"How do you feel?" we ask someone.

"I feel terrible," he replies, not realizing he has commanded his body to be sick.

"Can you do it?" we ask.

"I can't do that," he replies, not knowing he has limited God and himself by his words.

"I can't get out of debt," someone says. He has just commanded his debt to continue.[133]

6. Never make a negative confession.

We call such negative assertions [see number 5 above] "realistic appraisals" of the situation. But they aren't realistic, for they ignore the power of God, the authority of the invisible world of the spirit, and the grant of power made by God to his children.[134]

Robertson's basic agreement with the cultic positive confession movement is but one more indication of how much he opposes Biblical Christianity. What he advocates, and what the positive confession movement teaches, is indistinguishable from sorcery.

Extraordinary Divine Gifts Have Ceased

While Satanic miracles and ridiculous frauds continue in this supposedly enlightened twentieth century, the end of three sorts of divine miracles—tongues, prophesying, and words of knowledge—is explicitly taught in the Bible:

> Love never fails. But whether there are prophecies, they will fail; whether there are tongues, they will cease; whether there is knowledge, it will vanish away. For we know in part and we prophesy in part. But when that which is perfect has come, then that which is in part will be done away.
>
> When I was a child, I spoke as a child, I understood as a child, I thought as a child, but when I became a man, I put away childish things. For now we see in a mirror, dimly, but then face to face. Now I know in part, but then I shall know just as I also am known.[135]

Robertson claims to have received thousands of "words of knowledge," and to have spoken in tongues many times. Exactly what tongues are, we shall discuss in a moment. First, however, we must understand this bald Biblical assertion that tongues, knowledge, and prophecies will cease. When will they cease? If they have ceased already, then Robertson's religion is shown even more clearly to be false.

Paul says that they will cease when "that which is perfect has come." What is the "perfect"? In *Shout It From The Housetops* Robertson recounts this conversation he had with a local Baptist minister:

> Pulling out his Bible, the pastor continued, with just a trace of hostility in his voice, "My Bible says 'whether there be tongues, they shall cease . . . for when that which is perfect is come, that which is in part shall be done away.' The Bible was the perfect thing which came into this earth. And when it came, tongues passed away. They are not for today."
>
> This was not the first rejection of the supernatural power of God that I [Robertson] had run into, but I was, nonetheless, taken aback. However, the Holy Spirit is equal to all occasions, and I found myself answering, "Now, brother, I don't want to be argumentative about this matter. I've never made an issue of this and don't expect to, but that's just poor exegesis. That same passage from I Corinthians 13 says 'whether there be knowledge, it shall vanish away.' If tongues are not for today, then neither is knowledge. That passage refers to the second coming of Jesus, and no scholarly exegete will say otherwise."[136]

Robertson's seminary training was defective, as almost all seminary training is. He should have read the Baptist John Gill who explained in his commentary on 1 Corinthians more than two centuries ago, "the gift of speaking with diverse tongues will cease, indeed it has already." So at least one scholarly exegete did say otherwise. There have been many more.

But Robertson's scholarship is not only lacking, his understanding of this passage is impossible. If it refers, as he asserts, to Christ's Second Coming, then tongues and knowledge both must cease at the Second Coming. When Christ comes, in other words, our minds will be totally blank, and we shall stop speaking the "tongues of angels" when we meet them!

Fortunately, the Bible does not teach Eastern mysticism, and "that which is perfect" does not and cannot refer to Christ. Nor does "knowledge" refer to all knowledge. In 1 Corinthians 11:26 Paul refers to the Lord's Second Coming: "For as often as you eat this bread and drink this cup, you proclaim the Lord's death till He comes." If Paul had had the Second Coming in mind in 1 Corinthians 13, he could have used similar language. Two chapters later, in chapter 15, he refers to the "end."[137] Why does he not use that word in chapter 13 if he is referring to the end of the world?

The Greek word Paul used in 1 Corinthians 13 is in the neuter case. It is an "it." Christ is not an "it." The neuter case is reflected in the English translation as well: "that which is perfect," not "the one who is perfect." The Baptist preacher dimly recognized that, but it completely escaped Robertson. The word means literally, "the completed thing." The Greek word, *to teleion,* is used 18 times in the New Testament and never refers to the Second Coming of Christ.[138] The completed thing in 1 Corinthians 13 is the Bible, God's final revelation to His people.

In his selection of a word to describe the cessation of the gifts of tongues, knowledge, and prophesying, Paul chose *katargeo,* a very strong word which means *destroyed.* The same word is used in 1 Corinthians 15:26: "The last enemy that will be destroyed is death." The use of this word indicates that "the cessation of the prophetic gifts was to be a complete obliteration beyond recall. Paul left no room for any thought of temporary lapse and revival. If the prophetic gifts ever ceased, they ceased for all time. But that they did cease at one point or another is clear from history. Therefore they have ceased for all time."[139]

The next point is the word "knowledge" in Paul's statement,

"whether there is knowledge, it will vanish away." What Paul is referring to here is not full knowledge, which will never vanish away, either at the Second Coming or at the completion of the writing of the Bible, but the "word of knowledge," the partial revelation that the apostles received prior to the completion of Scripture. When the full revelation, the Bible, is completed, then there will be no more need of "words of knowledge." What Robertson believes to be words of knowledge in his experience are not from God, for God has said that they will cease when the last chapter of the Bible is written. The last chapter was written 1900 years ago. Robertson's voices do not come from God; they come from somewhere else.

There is one final point that needs to be discussed in this passage. It is Paul's assertion that "now we see in a mirror, dimly, but then face to face. Now I know in part, but then I shall know just as I also am known." Many people see in these words an assertion of seeing Christ face to face in Heaven. But that cannot be what those words mean.

The first half of Paul's sentence is clearly a metaphor: "we see in a mirror, dimly." It is obviously a figure of speech. He was not talking about literal mirrors or physical sight. But some people, while correctly understanding the first half of the sentence as a metaphor, a figure of speech, interpret the second half literally: They assert that *face to face* means literally face to face with Christ in Heaven. But that interpretation is not only inconsistent, it is not the way the Bible uses the phrase "face to face" in other passages. Notice how it is used in Numbers 12:6-8:

> Then He said, "Hear now My words: If there is a prophet among you, I, the Lord, make Myself known to him in a vision, and I speak to him in a dream. Not so with My servant Moses; he is faithful in all My house. I speak with him face to face, even plainly, and not in dark sayings; and he sees the form of the Lord.

To the ordinary prophets God revealed Himself in visions and dreams, but to Moses He speaks plainly, that is, face to face. The contrast is between dark sayings and plain speech. And that is also the contrast in 1 Corinthians 13. The gifts of prophecies, words of knowledge, and tongues were dark sayings compared to the clear and complete revelation made in Scripture. There is no suggestion that Heaven is the subject of Paul's passage. God's revelation to Moses took place on Earth. It was Moses who wrote the first five books of the Bible. Those books are the plain speech, the clear revelation, that God gave him.

In Exodus 33:9-11 we are given another instance of face to face revelation: "And it came to pass, when Moses entered the tabernacle, that the pillar of cloud descended and stood at the door of the tabernacle, and the Lord talked to Moses face to face, as a man speaks to his friend."[140]

In the ensuing conversation between Moses and God we are told:

> And he [Moses] said, "Please, show me Your glory."
> Then He said, "I will make all My goodness pass before you, and I will proclaim the name of the Lord before you. I will be gracious to whom I will be gracious, and I will have compassion on whom I will have compassion."
> But He said, "You cannot see My face; for no man shall see Me, and live."
> And the Lord said, "Here is a place by me, and you shall stand on the rock. So it shall be, while My glory passes by, that I will put you in the cleft of the rock, and will cover you with My hand while I pass by. Then I will take away My hand, and you shall see My back; but My face shall not be seen."

In Deuteronomy 34:10 we find the phrase again, and it reinforces our point: "But since then there has not arisen in Israel a prophet like Moses, whom the Lord knew face to face." God knew Moses "face to face," God spoke to Moses "face to face," yet we are told that Moses never saw God's face. The phrase is a figure of speech: God revealed Himself clearly and fully to Moses, unlike His revelation to the other prophets. And when the "perfect" comes, Paul is teaching in 1 Corinthians 13, we will know God face to face. Paul was an educated Israelite who knew the Old Testament well. He was using the phrase in the same sense that Moses used it: to contrast a partial revelation with a full one. It has nothing to do with seeing Jesus Christ literally face to face in Heaven.[141]

What Paul is teaching here in 1 Corinthians is that divine prophecy, tongues, and words of knowledge were temporary gifts given to the apostles and those whom they blessed. They were gifts only for the infancy of the church, and they would be destroyed when the final and complete revelation of God in the Bible was completed. Today there are no divine prophecies, but there are plenty of human and demonic ones.

Today there are no divine words of knowledge, but there are plenty of human and demonic ones. Today there are no divine tongues, but there are plenty of human and demonic tongues. Pat Robertson's prophecies and words of knowledge are either the result of his overwrought imagination, or the voices of demons which he mistakenly believes to be the voice of God. As we saw in chapter 3, he has made many mistakes in interpreting these voices in the past. It is just possible that his major mistake is thinking that God is talking to him at all.

Chapter Five
Twisting Scripture

Those who are untaught and unstable twist [Paul's letters] to their own destruction, as they do also the rest of the Scriptures.
2 Peter 3:16.

Central to Robertson's experiential religion is the baptism of the Holy Spirit and its principal manifestation, speaking in tongues. Robertson has spoken in tongues many times, both publicly and privately. To the listener, the sounds that come out of his mouth sound like gibberish, but he, like nearly all Charismatics, insists that he is speaking the tongues of angels. The tongues, nearly everyone agrees, are not human languages. If they are a language at all, they are languages that belong to angels.

Unfortunately the Charismatics seem not to have thought of the possibility that the sounds they make are the tongues of demons. Demons, after all, are merely evil angels, so the tongues of angels may refer to the tongues of fallen angels, that is, demons.

This possibility becomes even stronger when one understands that tongues-speaking is not limited to Charismatics or others who profess to be Christian. Like miracles and prophecies, tongues are frequently found among religions that Robertson himself would presumably acknowledge to be false. Richard Quebedeaux reports that "Speaking in tongues, spiritual healing, 'possession' by spirits, and prophetic utterances were common occurrences in the shamanistic traditions of Africa, Latin America, and elsewhere long before the birth of the pentecostal movement."[142] In Book VI of the *Aeneid*, Virgil reports a priestess on the island of Delos who achieved union with the god Apollo and would speak in unintelligible tongues. Chrysostom, the fourth century Greek theologian, describes the Pythoness at Delphi who "being in a frenzy [would] utter the words of her madness."[143] *The New Schaff-Herzog Encyclopedia of Religious Knowledge* reports that

> The Greek-Roman world furnishes many evident parallels. The Greek oracles were mediated through priests or priestesses who uttered what the divinity suggested to them while their consciousness was in complete abeyance. Another characteristic of the giving of oracles is the obscurity or unintelligibility of the oracle, which ever needs explication.[144]

Speaking in tongues is found among Mormons; one of the founders of the church, Brigham Young, spoke in tongues.[145] The seventh article of faith of the Church of Jesus Christ of Latter-Day Saints says that the Mormons "believe in the gifts of tongues, prophecy, revelation, visions, healing, [and] interpretation of tongues."[146] The whirling dervishes of Persia spoke in tongues. Religious Eskimos speak in tongues. Paul G. Hiebert reports that:

> The use of sacred languages and sounds is common in religious experience associated with trance or ecstasy, and is frequently linked with shamanism in tribal religions. There are numerous testimonies of healings and other miracles performed by the Virgin of Guadalupe, Tirupathi Venkateswara in South India, Voodoo spirits in Latin America, the Buddha, and many other gods, spirits, and healers. Even the use of the name "Jesus Christ" is no test of the presence of the Holy Spirit. This name is widely used in South American spiritism, and in syncretistic Hindu-Christian movements in India such as that led by Subba Rao of Andhra Pradesh. The fact is that spirit possession, feelings of ecstasy and joy, and resurrections are reported in all major religious systems.[147]

Ecstatic unintelligible utterance is not a monopoly of the Charismatics; it is a characteristic of many false religions. One would be hard pressed to find any significant difference between these pagan practices, modern day "channeling," speaking in Charismatic tongues, and "prophesying."

Biblical Tongues

All those phenomena, however, have nothing to do with Christianity or the Bible. There the tongues that were spoken were intelligible human languages:

> And they [the apostles] were all filled with the Holy Spirit and began to speak with other tongues, as the Spirit gave them utterance. Now there were dwelling in Jerusalem Jews, devout men, from every nation under heaven. And when this sound occurred, the multitude came together, and were confused, because everyone heard them speak in his own language .... "We hear them speaking in our own tongues the wonderful works of God."[148]

Now the Greek words translated in these verses as *tongues* are the same: *glossa*. This same word, from which we derive the English word *glossolalia*, occurs many times in 1 Corinthians 13 and 14 as well: "Though I speak with the tongues of men and of angels" (13:1); "For he who speaks in a tongue does not speak to men but to God" (14:2); "He who speaks in a tongue edifies himself" (14:4); "I wish you all spoke with tongues" (14:5); "he who prophesies is greater than he who speaks with tongues" (14:5); "if I come to you speaking with tongues" (14:6); "unless you utter by the tongue words easy to understand" (14:9); "Let him who speaks in a tongue" (14:13); "For if I pray in a tongue" (14:14); "I thank my God that I speak with tongues more than you all" (14:18); "I would rather speak five words with my understanding, that I may teach others also, than ten thousand words in a tongue" (14:19); "Of other tongues" (14:21); "tongues are for a sign not for those who believe" (14:22); "if the whole church comes together in one place, all speak with tongues" (14:23); "each of you ... has a tongue" (14:26); "If anyone speaks in a tongue" (14:27); and "do not forbid to speak with tongues" (14:39).

In every instance, the word means language; it does not mean gibberish. We are misled by our translations of the Bible, for the word *tongues* has come to mean unintelligible nonsense, rather than foreign languages. It means foreign languages, as we have seen from Acts 2.

Not only are Biblical "tongues" foreign languages, they are languages understood, though not studied, by their speakers. We are told in 1 Corinthians 14:4: "He who speaks in a tongue edifies himself." Yet no one can be edified or built up by something he does not understand. If I write or say, hrysdt gjhuti whweu, I have edified no one, least of all myself. The sounds and the "words" are unintelligible. They mean nothing. And if I speak Mandarin Chinese, and do not understand the words, then I am not built up either. But if I speak Mandarin Chinese, and understand what I am saying, then I can be edified. There can be no edification without understanding. Yet it is standard Charismatic teaching that the tongues speaker does not know what he is saying. All that is important is that he have the experience. But Christianity, unlike the Charismatic movement, insists on the primacy of truth and understanding, not experience. God has given us a propositional revelation which we are to study until we understand it.

Guidance

Pat Robertson uses the Bible as a Ouija board. Here are his own accounts of how he gets answers from the Bible.

Before his first religious experience, he says, ". . . I had been reading the Bible daily for the last year. In fact, on several occasions I had opened the Bible and had Scripture verses almost leap out at me as answers to my prayers."[149] When he was in Canada, trying to decide whether he should return to his pregnant wife, he

> sat down on a rock and looked out over the shimmering lake. "God, give me a word," I prayed. I let my Bible fall open. There on the page before me was his answer. "But I would have you without carefulness. He that is unmarried careth for the things that belong to the Lord, how he may please the Lord: But he that is married careth for the things that are of the world, how he may please his wife" (I Cor. 7:32).
>
> It was as if God were saying, "Put me ahead of your wife and I'll take care of your wife."[150]

When Robertson was deciding which seminary to go to, he

> opened the Bible and reached out and put my finger in the middle of one of the pages. I read the verse I was pointing at: "Say not ye, There are yet four months, and then cometh harvest? Behold, I say unto you, Lift up your eyes, and look on the fields; for they are white already to harvest" (John 4:35).

"You see," I almost shouted to Dede who was sitting there dumbfounded. "God doesn't want me to go all the way up to Gordon—he wants me to stay here."[151]

When Robertson was considering whether to buy a house in Brooklyn, he fasted and prayed in a church:

> There was a single sixty watt bulb‡ burning over the altar, and I went inside, sat cross-legged on the floor in the semidark auditorium, and prayed, "Lord, do you want us to buy that house and stay here?"
> Immediately I had an impression in my mind. "Jeremiah 16:2."
> "Is that what you said, God?" I asked out loud. "Did you say Jeremiah 16:2?"
> The impression stayed on my heart, even stronger. I reached for my Bible and thumbed through it until I found the sixteenth chapter of Jeremiah. I put my finger on the second verse and read: "Thou shalt not take thee a wife, neither shalt thou have sons or daughters in this place."
> I leaped to my feet and ran out of the building.[152]

While setting up his first television station Robertson learned the meaning of a prophecy he had received before leaving New York:

> Before we left New York I had received a Scripture prophecy which I never had understood, although I knew it applied to the TV station. The Scripture was I Kings 6:37. "In the fourth year was the foundation of the house of the Lord laid, in the month of Zif." Now as I remembered, the month of Zif on the Jewish calendar was the month of May. The foundations had at last been secured, and prophecy was fulfilled. Four years had gone by since I had given my life to Jesus Christ."[153]

The Scripture obviously referred to the establishment of the Christian Broadcasting Network.

After his father's defeat in the Democratic primary in 1966, Robertson again consulted the Bible:

---

‡ Robertson must have an extraordinary memory. He wrote this sentence at least ten years and perhaps 13 years after he was in the church. Yet he remembered that the bulb was sixty watts. On second thought, perhaps he doesn't have a good memory. Perhaps a voice told him how many watts were in the bulb.

I slipped from the bed and picked up my Bible and let it fall open. As in times past, God spoke to me through the Scriptures, and this time my eyes rested on I Samuel 16:1. "How long wilt thou mourn for Saul, seeing I have rejected him from reigning over Israel: fill thine horn with oil, and go . . . ."

Instantly I had peace.[154]

Robertson's use of Scripture illustrates exactly what he means when he tells people to read the Bible. He regards the Bible as sort of an electronic billboard on which messages flash for each reader. One verse can have an indefinite number of meanings. This writer presumes that few readers knew that 1 Corinthians 7:32 means "stay in Canada;" that John 4:53 means "do not go to Gordon Seminary;" that Jeremiah 16:2 means "leave New York;" that 1 Kings 6:37 refers to the organization of CBN in 1960; or that 1 Samuel 16:1 speaks about the 1966 Virginia Democratic Senatorial primary. Robertson's Bible is truly what the atheists have falsely accused the Christian Bible of being: a wax nose that can be interpreted to mean anything one wishes. This sort of misuse of Scripture is Satanic, for Satan himself quoted Scripture out of context and made arbitrary applications when he tempted Christ in the wilderness.

Despite Robertson's frequent references to the Bible, which becomes a wax nose in his hands, he refers far more often to his voices, his impressions, his hunches, and his experiences. The Bible plays quite a subsidiary role in guiding him. It is little more than a Ouija board for his finger to fall on to.

This attitude is not surprising. One of the principal dogmas of the Charismatic movement is its emphasis on experience, and its neglect of a serious study of the Bible. Robertson explains his superstitious method of misusing the Bible in his books. On the subject of guidance he writes:

> God's primary means for giving us guidance is the Bible. The Bible is our rulebook of faith and practice. If we know and understand the scriptures, we will be well on our way to having His guidance. He never guides His people contrary to the clear principles of His written Word.
> Second, guidance comes from a knowledge of God Himself [notice: knowledge of the Bible is not a knowledge of God.] We need to know what pleases Him and what displeases Him. There is no substitute [note well] for walking with God, sharing with him, and talking to Him daily. When you do that, you will experience His direction and His correction. You will

Twisting Scripture / 65

come to know what his desire is . . . .
  Finally, to have His guidance, you need to be filled with his Spirit. The Bible says, "As many as are led by the Spirit of God, these are the Sons of God." Jesus said that the Holy Spirit will lead you into all truth. In the book of Acts, there are recorded instances where the Holy Spirit gave personal guidance. He said to do this or not to do that. He gave revelations. And He still does all these things! He guides by means of specific scriptures that suddenly come alive for you. He guides by bringing people to you providentially to give you advice and counsel. He guides through circumstances. But you must be filled with the Spirit.[155]
  The best way to know God's will is to be familiar with the Bible. That is because virtually everything you need to know concerning the will of God is in the Bible . . . .
  Another way you can know the will of God is through prayer, when you commune with God and learn what pleases Him . . . . I would say emphatically that the Bible and the peace that comes about through a continuous relationship with God are the best ways of knowing His will.
  It is true that God will show us His will through a number of other means. He will show us His will through godly counselors. We can know His will in part through circumstances. We can also know the will of God through the inner voice of the Spirit as God speaks to us. Sometimes God will send us visions or dreams. He may send us angels or even appear to us Himself.[156]

All these experiences, these means of guidance, are necessary because Robertson believes that the Bible is imperfect. He does not elaborate on the nature of its alleged imperfection. He does not say whether it contains errors or myths. It is unimportant to him whether an historical passage in the Bible is true or not. Read carefully what he says:

  Many people teach that miracles stopped at the end of the first century when the last apostle died. Those people misinterpret I Corinthians 13:8 which says, "Whether there are prophecies, they will fail; whether there are tongues, they will cease; whether there is knowledge, it will vanish away." The chapter goes on to say that when the perfect has come, the imperfect will be taken away. Some say "the perfect" is the Bible.
  There is only one that is perfect, Jesus Christ.[157]

  I believe it [the story of Adam and Eve in Genesis] is real. It is as good an explanaiton of what happened as there could be. . . . It does not offend my reason to think there was one original couple that God made, and that from this couple came all the other people on the earth. Nor would my faith be shattered if one day I learned that this story was an allegorical description of God's creation of man.[158]

All of this is antithetical to what the Bible says about itself. In one of his great passages explaining the significance of Christ's death and resurrection, the apostle Paul draws a parallel between Adam and Christ.[159] They are the first Adam and the Last, or second, Adam.[160] Now if Adam were possibly allegorical, then perhaps Christ was as well. Indeed, Luke's entire genealogy of Christ traces his ancestry back to Adam,[161] who, according to Robertson, future scholarship may show to be a myth. This comment by Robertson shows how far his religion is independent of history. It would not shatter his faith to learn that Adam was an allegory. Would a legendary Noah, or an allegorical Abraham, or a mythical Moses shatter his faith? Perhaps Christ Himself will turn out to be an allegory. When one bases one's religion on experience, history and the Bible become irrelevant.

This attitude is foreign to Scripture. Emphasizing history, the apostle Paul said, "If Christ is not risen, your faith is futile; you are still in your sins!"[162] The Psalmist, emphasizing the importance of Scripture, wrote, "Your word is a lamp to my feet and a light to my path."[163] "Direct my steps by Your word, and let no iniquity have dominion over me."[164] Paul, emphasizing Scripture, said that the Bible completely equips the man of God for every good work. He does not need to seek a sign from God; he has a book to read, study, understand, and believe. That book tells about God and his work in history. But an evil and adulterous generation seeks after a sign, according to Christ.[165]

Asking the question, "How can I know the will of God?" is a fundamental mistake that many people, not just Pat Robertson, make. One can know the commands of God in the Bible. They apply to every situation in life. But the will of God, God's purpose for our lives, cannot be known. Deuteronomy 29:29 says, "The secret things belong to the Lord our God, but those things which are revealed belong to us and to our children forever, that we may do all the words of the law."

The heathen nations consult their fortunetellers, their oracles, their tea leaves, and their astrologers, trying to discover the will of their gods for their lives. There is no difference between what they do, and what Pat Robertson does—at least no difference that makes Pat Robertson's practices superior to theirs. The fact that he uses the Bible rather than a Ouija board makes his practice more objectionable, for he is scorning the Word of God while pretending to find hidden meanings in it intended for himself alone. Robertson has the Bible, and he rejects it. He does not trust God with his whole heart; he leans on his own understanding, or, more precisely, his own imagination.

Several years ago, when this writer worked for a Member of Congress, the Congressman received a letter from a woman in Texas. This is what the woman wrote:

> A year ago last January, I unfortunately found myself in the position of being pregnant and knowing I could not have the child. I elected to have an abortion because I was making less than $1,200 per month at the time and knew I could not support myself and a child. I did not want to attempt to go on welfare because I believe that anyone who can work should. No one on the face of this earth can say whether or not I committed murder. ONLY God can or can't. I prayed and prayed for guidance and I found I was led to have the abortion. After the act, I felt very guilty and very depressed. I went to visit a Presbyterian minister who sat and talked with me. He did not condemn or condone. He explained that modern religion had unfortunately adopted the view of situations only having black or white sides with no gray areas. He told me that he served on the board of an agency dealing with mentally retarded children and, in his opinion, it was more of a sin to put these children away to be forgotten rather than to have had them never born. I think about my child often and wonder what he or she would be like. But, I know that my baby is much better off in heaven with God than on earth with me. Unless you have been through this situation, which obviously you have not, you can never know what it is like to go through with the act. The Bible warns us not to judge lest we be judged.

Notice how the murder is justified: "I prayed and prayed for guidance and I found I was led to have the abortion." The murder is directly attributable to the notion that guidance from God is to be sought outside the pages of the Bible. It is Pat Robertson's theology of direct "leading" from God, combined with the idea of an imperfect Bible, that killed this baby. Many times professing Christians will thoughtlessly say that "God has led them to do" something, that "God has given them peace," that "It is God's will for me" and so forth. All such statements are both impious and false. One should not blame one's actions on God.[166]

The Sovereignty of God

After the doctrine of Scripture, which is the most fundamental doctrine of Christianity, the most important doctrine is the doctrine of God. If one makes a serious mistake on either of these two doctrines, he has lost the whole of Christianity. Robertson, as we have seen, rejects what the Bible says about itself. He also rejects what it says about God.

The fundamental lesson to be learned about God is that He is *God.* He is the Creator; we are His creatures. He is all-powerful, all-knowing, all-present. In the words of the *Westminster Confession of Faith,*

> There is but one only living and true God, who is infinite in being and perfection, a most pure spirit, invisible, without body, parts, or passions, immutable, immense, eternal, incomprehensible, almighty, most wise, most holy, most free, most absolute, working all things according to the counsel of his own immutable and most righteous will, for his own glory; most loving, gracious, merciful, long-suffering, abundant in goodness and truth, forgiving iniquity, transgression and sin; the rewarder of them that diligently seek him; and withal most just and terrible in his judgments; hating all sin, and who will by no means clear the guilty . . . .[167]

One must contrast this Biblical description of God with the God that Robertson portrays, a God who is a servant to the wishes, whims, and wills of men: "At any rate, He revealed Himself to the covenant people as I AM. It was almost like a blank check. God said, "I am _____," and His people were to fill in the blank according to their need."[168]

But God is not here to meet our needs, like a cosmic butler or nurse. Rather, we are here for His purposes and for His glory.

> Behold, the nations are as a drop in a bucket, and are counted as the small dust on the balance; look, He lifts up the isles as a very little thing. And Lebanon is not sufficient to burn, nor its beasts sufficient for a burnt offering. All nations before Him are as nothing, and they are counted by Him less than nothing and worthless . . . .
> It is He who sits above the circle of the earth, and its inhabitants are

like grasshoppers, who stretches out the heavens like a curtain, and spreads them out like a tent to dwell in. He brings the princes to nothing; He makes the judges of the earth useless.[169]

I am the Lord, and there is no other; there is no God besides Me. I will gird you, though you have not known Me, that they may know from the rising of the sun to its setting that there is none besides Me. I am the Lord, and there is no other; I form the light and create darkness, I make peace and create evil; I, the Lord, do all these things.[170]

But Robertson denies that God is the creator of all things:

> First of all, God does not cause evil. Evil is a result of two major forces: the first force is a being named *Satan*....
> [T]he second source of evil is the *human heart*.[171]

Now the Bible nowhere teaches that evil is a result of two major forces. Such an idea contradicts the Bible's explicit claims that God is the creator of all things, including evil. I have already quoted Isaiah 45:7 on this point; Lamentations 3:38 says: "Is it not from the mouth of the most high that woe [evil] and well-being proceed?" There is no dualism in the universe. Satan is not the equal of God, but one of God's creatures. But Robertson sees in Satan and man two forces that can frustrate the will and the purposes of God.

> When God allows Satan a certain amount of leeway, He is permitting the exercise of free will on the part of one of His created beings.[172]
>
> If God did not give men the chance to be evil, there would be no freedom.... Giving man the freedom to choose between good and evil has been God's policy since he created the first man, Adam.[173]
>
> In the beginning, Adam was morally neutral. He was able to choose to sin—and he was able to choose not to sin. Adam's sin predisposed all of his descendants toward evil. Therefore, we all have a tendency that pulls us toward sin.
>
> Although we have a predisposition toward sin and evil, we can turn away from sin and turn toward God.[174]
>
> Babies who are not baptized will not go to hell because they are not guilty of anything.... Babies have not done anything wrong because they do not know the difference between right and wrong. And so they have not sinned.[175]
>
> If it were not possible to live a holy life, God would not have commanded it.[176]

To reply to this last statement first, perhaps God commanded us to live a holy life in order to teach us that we cannot do so, and that we need a Savior. That is what Christianity teaches. The law is a schoolmaster to drive us to Christ.[177] But Robertson teaches that a man may save himself. It follows logically that man has no need of a Savior. Robertson's theology is humanism in religious clothing.[178] It is also extremely poor logic. It simply does not follow that because God commands something, it can be done. Not only may God have other purposes in commanding it, one cannot derive a factual conclusion from an imperative premise.

Free will, that is, a will independent of God, is another superstition not taught in the Bible. The Bible teaches that "the king's heart is in the hand of the Lord, like the rivers of water; He turns it wherever He wishes."[179] And if a king's heart is in the hand of God, surely a television broadcaster's heart is there too.

Nor does man have the freedom to choose between good and evil. Such a position, advanced in the early church by the heretic Pelagius, was condemned by Augustine, who quoted Paul quoting the Old Testament:

> There is none righteous, no, not one; there is none who understands; there is none who seeks after God. They have all gone out of the way; they have together become unprofitable; there is none who does good, no, not one. Their throat is an open tomb; with their tongues they have practiced deceit; the poison of asps is under their lips, whose mouth is full of cursing and bitterness. Their feet are swift to shed blood; destruction and misery are in their ways; and the way of peace they have not known. There is no fear of God before their eyes.[180]

The Bible does not teach that man has a mere "predisposition" to sin; it teaches that all men, including babies, are actually sinners: "For all have sinned and fall short of the glory of God."[181] The Psalmist lamented, "Behold, I was brought forth in iniquity, and in sin my mother conceived me."[182] Nor does the Bible teach that Adam was created "morally neutral." God pronounced His entire creation, including Adam, "very good."[183]

Robertson's low view of God complements his high view of man, for he simultaneously denigrates God and exalts man. Man can not only frustrate God's plan by exercising his uncontrollable free will, but man is not nearly as bad as the Bible says:

Original sin is a theological term that goes back to the fall of man. As I said before, man was created in God's image, righteous [this is surprising; Robertson had just said that man was created morally neutral] and free. He was a free moral agent, freely able to choose God or turn away from Him. By eating the fruit of the tree of the knowledge of good and evil, he did the one thing he was asked [!] not to do . . . .

From that moment on, the spirit of man was damaged. It is as if man is now born with a moral handicap. He is lame in the most important part of his being—his spirit.[184]

We should keep in mind that original sin is a tendency to do evil, not an act of evil. Guilt comes when we commit acts of evil. There is no such thing as "original guilt." God does not punish people for tendencies, only for what they do in light of what they know. Therefore, little babies do not go to hell because of original sin, because babies have never committed any sinful acts.[185]

But the Bible does not say that man is "lame" in sin; it says that he is dead in sin. In Robertson's theology, morally, man has a sprained ankle. According to the Bible, morally, man has rigor mortis. The Bible says that all our righteousnesses are as filthy rags.

The Bible also says that all men are guilty: "Whatever the law says, it says to those who are under the law, that every mouth may be stopped, and all the world may become guilty before God."[186] Paul asserts that "through one man sin entered the world, and death through sin, and thus death spread to all men, because all sinned."[187] Robertson's views of God and man have no support whatsoever in the Bible. His distinction between original sin and original guilt is both un-Biblical and contradictory: How can one have original sin and not be guilty? By his account, Christ could have been tainted by original sin, and yet be sinless.

Because Robertson's god is a limited god, not the almighty God of the Bible, he views suffering as an unintended consequence of God's creation of natural laws: "Such suffering [caused by the operations of natural laws] does not result from God's intentions, but comes rather from man's foolishness."[188]

But the Bible teaches that God intends whatever happens; that neither Satan, nor man, nor natural law operate independently of His will, nor do they cause results that He did not intend. "In whom also we have obtained an inheritance, being predestined according to the purpose of Him who works all things according to the counsel of His will."[189] God has made all things for Himself.[190]

For His dominion is an everlasting dominion, and His kingdom is from generation to generation. All the inhabitants of the earth are reputed as nothing; He does according to His will in the army of heaven and among the inhabitants of the earth. No one can restrain His hand or say to Him, "What have You done?"[191]

Despite the unmistakable clarity of the Bible's teaching that God causes and controls everything that happens, Robertson persists in saying such things as, "God did not send herpes. It is a natural consequence of immorality . . . ."[192] But in the Bible there is no "nature" that operates apart from God's intentions and purposes. The concept of "nature" is foreign to the Bible. There is the Creator, and there are the creatures, and nothing happens among the hosts of heaven or the inhabitants of the earth that God did not plan or intend.

Robertson, however, insists that God neither plans nor controls all things:

> Why does God allow this to happen? When we ask this question, it brings us back to the statement that God has created man as a free being—free even to the point of ruining much of God's creation.[193]
>
> Those who hurt must remember that it is not God's will for anyone to suffer.[194]

Such a statement is preposterous, given the many statements in Scripture where God's intention that people suffer is unequivocally set forth. It was God's will that Job suffer enormous losses of wealth, health, and family.[195] It was God's will that Paul should suffer in order to keep him from becoming conceited.[196] It was God's will that Jonah suffer in order to teach him a lesson about God's mercy.[197] It is God's will that Christians suffer in order to produce patience and humility.[198] It was God's will that the man be born blind in order that God might be glorified.[199] It is God's will that Christians should suffer in order to correct their errors and sins.[200] This list of passages from the Bible could be extended indefinitely. To say, as Robertson does, that "it is not God's will for anyone to suffer," is ludicrous. It reveals a man who is either profoundly ignorant of, or profoundly in disagreement with, the Bible.

Predestination

Robertson admits that his belief in free will contradicts what the Bible teaches about predestination, but he insists that the Bible teaches free will as well. Rather than questioning his interpretation of Scripture, which results in attributing a contradiction to the Bible, Robertson asserts that there is a "tension," that is, a contradiction in Scripture.

> The Bible tells us definitely that God knows everything. Furthermore we are told that God has planned (or predestined) certain things. [The Bible says that God has predestined all things.—JWR] We were chosen in Christ from the foundation of the earth. So if God knows everything, and He also has the ability to control everything, then how, indeed, can we have free will? Doesn't God have to work it all out in advance? The answer to that is no.
>
> His foreknowledge could be likened to a motion picture. If we watch a movie we see the frames in sequence, so it looks as if Act 2 follows Act 1 and Act 3 follows Act 2. We see what looks like consecutive action. But if you were to take that same piece of film and hang it up on the wall, you could see the end, the beginning, and the middle all at once. You really would not have to control the action in order to see what was going to happen. In an imperfect sense this illustrates how God's foreknowledge and our free will can coexist. Yet there are dimensions of life that are beyond our understanding. The concept of predestination and foreknowledge, as opposed to free will, makes up one of those dimensions . . . .
>
> There seems to be a tension between two ostensibly irreconcilable points: the free will of man, and the foreknowledge and predestination of God . . . . There is not some timeless, immutable decree from God that governs man, but constant, loving help and direction from Him . . . .[201]

Now those who believe in free will seem strangely compelled to offer illustrations to explain what they mean. The usual illustration involves an observer on a hill high above an intersection, toward which two cars are speeding. The observer "knows" that the two cars will collide, but his knowledge does not cause them to collide.

Robertson offers a fresh illustration that is, if possible, even more inept than the high hill imagery. Does God see the future in the mirror of His own will? Where else could He see it? And if God knows, not just guesses, but knows what will happen, then that event must happen. Otherwise, God did not know it. Yet the one thing Robertson is sure about is that "there is not some timeless immutable decree from God that governs man." He asserts this with such vehemence that one can only conclude that he finds the idea of the sovereignty of God repugnant.

Salvation

Robertson's thoroughly un-Christian views of God and man lead to a peculiar doctrine of salvation. He writes, "The Bible teaches that all people are beloved by God and that they all have an equal chance . . . ."[202] Now the Bible teaches no such thing. It does teach that "Faith comes by hearing, and hearing by the word of God."[203] It also teaches that without faith it is impossible to please God.[204] But there are millions now dead who never heard the word of God. Did they have an equal chance? Did Christ die for them? Was Judas beloved by God? If all people are beloved by God, why does God say, "Jacob I have loved, but Esau I have hated"?[205] Does not Proverbs say that God has made the wicked for the day of evil?[206] And does not Paul teach that some people are "vessels of wrath fitted for destruction"?[207]

Furthermore, Robertson teaches salvation by works. Here is his summary of salvation:

> First, God says, "You are righteous by faith," then He gives you the Holy Spirit so that you can live righteously. Once you have been born again, you live the righteous demands of the law by the leading of the Holy Spirit. This is the process of regeneration that turns a sinner into a saint, fit for God's kingdom . . . .[208]

Robertson's account is a complete perversion of what the Bible teaches. First, regeneration is not a process, but an instantaneous event. It is the "new birth," which occurs once, and then is finished.

Second, no man, including the Christian, can live the righteous demands of the law. No man is saved by keeping the works of the law. He is saved only on account of Christ's obedience, not his own. Robertson denies the Reformation principles of *sola scriptura*—the Bible alone, *sola fide*—faith alone, *solo Christo*—Christ alone, and *sola gratia*—grace alone. He teaches a works righteousness that is condemned in the strongest possible terms by the apostle Paul in his letter to the Galatians.

Robertson places the ground of our salvation on the works that we do. It is not the historical Christ whose works save us, but the subjective "Christ," the "Christ" within, whose works we do.

> Just as the indwelling Spirit reproduces the life of Jesus, the outpoured, or baptizing, Spirit reproduces the ministry of Jesus....
>
> When we give ourselves to Jesus, the Holy Spirit comes to live within us. The Holy Spirit places us into Jesus. In turn Jesus immerses us in the power of the Holy Spirit, and from this experience comes the ability to reproduce the works of Jesus, including miracles and healings.[209]

In the final analysis, Robertson's religion is so totally man-centered that the Christ who saves is the "Christ" within.

Chapter 6
Playing Politics

For what will it profit a man if he gains the whole world, and loses his own soul?

Mark 8:36.

Pat Robertson's major decisions, and many of his minor decisions as well, have been made, he says, under the direct instruction of God. In chapter 3 we catalogued the alleged divine guidance he received when he was deciding whether to buy a house in Brooklyn, which seminary to attend, what the call letters of his television stations should be, how much money he should pay for it, which hymns to sing in church, whether to keep Jim Bakker on his staff, whether to return from Canada to help his pregnant wife, how much land to buy for his university, how much to pay for it, how much to pay RCA for new television equipment and so on.

It is not surprising, then, when Robertson tells us that he is running for President under the direct leading of God. It is hardly conceivable that he would make any minor decision, let alone a major one, without making such a claim to divine guidance. Speaking of his primary campaign in Michigan, Robertson said, "We saw the hand of God going before us in Michigan, affirming our every step."[210] In response to a question posed by *Christianity Today*, Robertson again asserted the blessing of God on his campaign:

> In the past, God has directed you to do various things, such as start CBN. Has he given you specific guidance regarding a presidential bid?

> I have received a leading similar to what I had when I came to Virginia Beach to start CBN.[211]

At another time Robertson said to his supporters:

> I have made the decision. Now it's up to you . . . . It was not an easy decision. It was not a quick decision. It was a decision made by careful, deliberate process over the course of two full years . . . two years of waiting on the Lord, listening to His voice . . . . Most important of all, I have made this decision in response to the clear and distinct promptings of the Lord's Spirit. I have walked with the Lord for more than 25 years. I know His voice. I know this is His direction. I know this is His will for my life. I am committed to it.[212]

The Arrogance of Fanatics

When a candidate is falsely convinced that God has told him to run for office, he tends to become a trifle arrogant with those who oppose him.

> Look at his [Robertson's] response to [U.S. Representative Jack] Kemp when he [Robertson] disagreed with the Representative's call for stronger sanctions against South Africa's racist government: "I am a prophet of God. God himself will fight for me against you—and He will win."[213]

The arrogance of this attitude, which makes God himself a Robertson campaign worker, is not characteristic of a true prophet of God. Robertson took the same "prophet of God" stance in a letter that he wrote to Norman Lear, head of People for the American Way, a leftist lobbying organization. This arrogance of the Charismatics, including Robertson, is what caused the PTL scandal, and it has been the plague of the Roman Catholic church for 1500 years.

Cecil M. Robeck, Jr., an instructor at Fuller Theological Seminary, a Charismatic and liberal seminary in California, noticed this problem when he was talking to a Charismatic leader in Great Britain:

> Recently, I asked a leader of charismatic renewal in Great Britain what he considered the greatest pastoral problem confronting the

charismatic movement. Without hesitation he remarked that within the movement there had emerged a few leaders who were no longer willing to submit their prophetic words to any form of testing. In essence they argued that their personal authority as proven "prophets" was all that was necessary for others to accept what they spoke "in the Spirit."[214]

Another observer notes that Charismatic "leaders often see themselves as above the norms, spiritual exercises and disciplines they impose upon their followers. And they reserve for themselves the right to interpret the Scriptures. The result is movements in which glory is given to leaders."[215]

An example of the arrogance of Charismatic musicians appeared in John MacArthur's *The Charismatics: A Doctrinal Perspective*. Bill and Gloria Gaither, well known, well paid, and widely respected recording artists, wrote and performed a song called *The King Is Coming*. When someone asked them for a theological interpretation of the song, he received this reply from their secretary:

> Regarding the interpretation of the song, "The King Is Coming," of all songs that song has been a gift from God. Bill and Gloria do not profess to be theologians. The song came quickly to them and they do not care to discuss the theology of it. In fact, they feel that to dissect the song would be tampering with the inspiration of the Holy Spirit who inspired the song.[216]

This attitude ought to be compared with Luke's attitude about the Jews at Berea: When the apostle Paul and Silas preached to them, the Jews searched the Scriptures daily, comparing what the apostle said with what Scripture says: "These were more fairminded than those in Thessalonica, in that they received the word with all readiness, and searched the Scriptures daily to find out whether these things were so."[217]

But the Charismatic "prophets" demand unquestioned obedience from their followers. Followers who have not been "anointed" are not supposed to interpret the Bible except as the "anointed" Charismatic leaders decree. This, of course, is identical to the old Roman Catholic denial of the right of private interpretation of Scriptures, a right granted in the Scriptures themselves. It is a characteristic of those who seek ecclesiastical and political power that they deny any limitation on their power, whether the limitation be the Bible or the Constitution.

Robertson and Politics

Robertson has never held political office in his life. He has been a lifelong Democrat ("I was a member of the Democratic Party for 55 years. . . . My father served in Congress for 34 years and was a lifetime Democrat. I supported Adlai Stevenson in 1952 and 1956"[218]), and he became a Republican only in 1985. His extraordinary attempt to leap from citizen to President of the United States runs afoul of one of "God's laws" as Robertson explains it in one of his books:

> In politics, the person who has successfully run for a city council seat is more likely to succeed in a race for mayor than someone who is unknown and untested. The mayor is then in a stronger position to move to the state legislature than the beginner, and on up the line to governor, senator, and perhaps president.[219]
>
> To want full accomplishment immediately is lust. It is a sin and calls for violation of the pattern of God. . . .
>
> So many well-meaning people have in fact done harm to individuals and indeed to nations by short-cutting God's plan and short-circuiting the blessings intended. . . .
>
> God's way is the way of gradual, sure growth and maturity, moving toward perfection.[220]

This, of course, is not the first of his own rules that Robertson has violated. He has repeatedly failed his test designed to distinguish a true prophet from a false one. Could it be that Robertson is not only a false prophet, but one beset by lust for power? Could Pat Robertson be one of those "well-meaning people" who have "done harm to individuals and nations by short-cutting God's plan"? Could he be a "sinner" who is "violating God's pattern"? It certainly appears so. But, of course, we are presuming that Charismatic leaders are subject to the same rules that they impose on their followers. That presumption may be entirely wrong.

Robertson's views about politics in general seem to have changed over the years. For example, in the September 1980 issue of *Pat Robertson's Perspective,* he wrote:

> A note about the upcoming elections and Christians in politics: . . . The Christian's chance to lead our nation is not through the levers of political power, but through service to its people and godly example.[221]
>
> Christians must avoid the temptation to win advantage by linking God's eternal program with the progress of temporal political parties. . . .
>
> An even greater danger to the church lies not in entering political battles, but in winning them.[222]

Those earlier views seem to have been forgotten in the excitement evoked by "God's leading."

Robertson's Political Views

Many of those who will be supporting Pat Robertson for President are political conservatives. Some of those conservatives do not share Robertson's belief in voices, miracles, and the value of gibberish, but they, nevertheless, deem politics more important than theology, and will vote for a conservative candidate. It is necessary, therefore, for anyone who supports Robertson to be familiar with his political views as well as his theological views. We can do no better than to quote his own words.

Pat Robertson favors the repudiation of the national debt; the cancellation of all debts, private and public, every fifty years; he favors a massive redistribution of property; he supports public education, an international police force, and the military draft.

In domestic policy, Robertson has made one major proposal: instituting a Year of Jubilee in America. In January 1981 Robertson proposed that the U.S. adopt the following Constitutional amendment: "At the end of every 49 years would be a 50th year of Jubilee. In the year of Jubilee, all debts would be cancelled."[223] He argues that "God's way is every 50 years to have a Jubilee and cancel all debts . . . that is the only way to solve the recession and national debt."[224]

> If inflation is to be broken, there must be a cancellation of debt—on a worldwide basis. Every type of debt, secured and unsecured, should be totally released. Government debt should be cancelled along with private debt. Contracts, leases, and similar obligations would have to be rewritten to accommodate a new set of economic conditons.
>
> Along with cancellation of debt would come the issuance of new

currency. To insure some type of fiscal discipline, new paper money should be freely convertible into some recognized standard of value—be it gold, silver, oil, coal, grain, or some combination thereof.

Obviously there would have to be a plan to inject new funds into the banking system so that depositors could get their money when needed. Provision would have to be made for adequate pension coverage for the elderly. New funding for insurance companies and similar financial institutions would be required. When the process was over, debt would be gone and along with it inflation and bogus paper money. The rich would still be rich and the poor would be poor, but all people would be released from bondage to unsupportable debt. The governments of the world would have been released from the throttlehold of money lenders, and the people would once again be in charge of their governments.[225]

The repudiation of the national debt is not a unique solution to the massive national debt problem, for certain anarchists have advocated the repudiation of the federal debt for years. But such a repudiation would be an enormously immoral act, accomplishing at once what the present program of government-induced inflation is achieving gradually. If it is immoral to reduce one's debts by debasing the monetary unit in which they are denominated, it is even more immoral to refuse to pay those debts altogether. At least the present system gives those who have lent money to the government some return on their contracts.

Robertson's plan would abrogate millions of private contracts too, not just those to which the federal government is a party. It would render void all loan agreements, installment plans, and mortgage loans that happen to extend into the Jubilee year.

Robertson's Jubilee proposal includes far more than the repudiation of the national debt and the cancellation of all private debts. He advocates the issuance of a new convertible paper currency by the government, the injection of new funds into the banking system, new funding for insurance companies, and new pension plans for the elderly.

Robertson seems to have derived this zany, immoral, and disastrous policy proposal from both rightwing and leftwing liberation theology, represented by the Reconstruction movement and Evangelicals for Social Action respectively.[226] Both of these versions of liberation theology teach that the Jubilee law of ancient Israel ought to be imposed on the United States. That law is stated in Leviticus 25:8-55. Among other things, such as the freeing of slaves, the Jubilee law required that the ancient tribal lands of Israel revert to their original owners or their children every fifty years. It was designed to maintain the integrity of the tribal territories assigned by God in ancient Israel.

The United States, of course, is not ancient Israel, nor does it have tribal territories assigned by God. Yet some people, on reading the Old Testament, have come to the conclusion that all the laws that applied to ancient Israel ought to apply to the United States as well. They insist, misunderstanding Scripture, that every "jot and tittle" of the law is or ought to be still in force. Some of these people believe that the United States is the New Israel; others believe that America is the promised land; still others believe that white people are God's chosen race; some simply like the idea of redistributing property; and some believe that the laws of ancient Israel are still obligatory on all nations, ancient and modern. Presumably these people would have us reinstitute stoning as a means of capital punishment and outlaw synthetic fabrics as well.

All such views are both false and un-Biblical. The Biblical view of God's law is summarized in the *Westminster Confession of Faith:*

> God gave to Adam a law, as a covenant of works, by which he bound him, and all his posterity, to personal, entire, exact, and perpetual obedience; . . .
>
> This law, after his fall, continued to be a perfect rule of righteousness; and, as such, was delivered by God upon Mount Sinai in ten commandments, and written in two tables; the first four commandments containing our duty towards God, and the other six our duty to man.
>
> Besides this law, commonly called moral, God was pleased to give to the people of Israel, as a church under age, ceremonial laws. . . . All which ceremonial laws are now abrogated under the New Testament.
>
> To them also, as a body politic, he gave sundry judicial laws, which expired together with the state of that people, not obliging any other now, further than the general equity thereof may require. . . .
>
> The moral law doth for ever bind all. . . . Neither does Christ in the gospel any way dissolve, but much strengthen this obligation.[227]

Robertson, however, mindlessly latches onto a law intended only for ancient Israel—a law which, by the way, there is no record of ancient Israel ever obeying—and urges that it be applied to the United States. Does he also intend to divide the American people into tribes, the territory of the United States into tribal homelands, and then relocate the newly designated tribes to their newly designated homelands? One supposes that he will hear the "voice of God" on all this as well.

Opposing Capitalism

> God set up a year of jubilee for his people to counteract the fact that a few eventually gain control of all wealth and land. In short, He directed that every fifty years all debt be canceled, all accumulated property be redistributed, and the cycle of use begin again. . . .[228]

> So a wise God decreed in Israel that there would be neither money loaned at interest nor perpetual debt. At the end of every 49 years there would be a 50th year of Jubilee. In the year of Jubilee, all debts would be cancelled, all slaves would be freed, and the means of production would be redistributed.[229]

Many socialists of the nineteenth and twentieth centuries have advocated plans to redistribute "all accumulated property" and to cancel "all debt." But few Presidential candidates who have run as "conservatives" have had the audacity to do so. Conservatives generally have opposed plans to redistribute wealth and property, and have championed the integrity of contracts. Those positions are Biblically correct, and the economic repercussions of the sort of redistributionist scheme that Robertson advocates would be devastating. Even in ancient Israel, all property was not redistributed. Leviticus 25:29-30 exempts urban property from such a redistribution, for example.

Robertson's hostility toward free enterprise comes through in this passage from his books:

> Although capitalism can be abused and abusive, it is the economic system most conducive to freedom, most in accord with human nature, and most closely related to the Bible. The unfettered *laissez-faire* concept of Adam Smith led to the free-booting robber barons of the nineteenth century. The story of the Rockefellers, the Vanderbilts, and other monopolistic capitalists, who built up the industrial base of our nation but who did so at the expense of their competitors, is not a pretty one. . . .
>
> Yes, unbridled capitalism must be restrained, or people will get too much money and too much power and will use it to oppress others.
>
> And the Bible contains a solution to the problem of excess accumulation of wealth and power. It is the year of Jubilee.[230]

Robertson sees the Jubilee as the redistributionist solution to the evils of capitalism. He has deeply drunk of the brew of economic interventionism, so popular earlier in this century. Presumably he learned such ideas at Yale. There is now a plethora of books on the economic history of the United States and Great Britain, but Robertson displays no acquaintance with them. They show that the abuses of power that occurred in the nineteenth century and are still occurring in the twentieth were abuses of political, not economic, power. The market, when not manipulated by politicians as Robertson advocates, is a system of countervailing forces that benefits its participants. But when political power can be used to gain an advantage—a monopoly in rail service, for example—then we are speaking no longer of "unbridled capitalism," but of bridled capitalism, which is exactly what Robertson advocates. His policies would make the abuses far worse, not better. What we need is not more redistribution of wealth, but less; not more interference in the market through regulations and taxes, but less; not bigger government, but a government tied down by the chains of the Constitution—and the Bible.

Robertson's views of economic history are twaddle, taken from the Communist Karl Marx, the interventionist John Maynard Keynes, and the Russian economist N.D. Kondratieff, an economic cycles fortune-teller:

> In our capitalistic Western society we have a redistribution mechanism called a depression. Every fifty to fity-six years, the accumulation of debt becomes insupportable, and the normal free market mechanisms fail to function. . . .
>
> Society, in a sense, starts over again. Our way of doing it is very painful. The biblical year of Jubilee is something that our society ought to learn. Otherwise we will be faced very shortly with a major crash and a depression.[231]

But a question arises: How could a major crash and depression be any worse than the massive redistribution of property and wealth that Robertson advocates? Does he seriously suppose that the Jubilee redistribution of "all accumulated property" and cancellation of "all debt" could be executed painlessly? His proposal would ensure economic collapse, for he would outlaw the free market by force.

Robertson also seems to be a bit of a Luddite:

> The technological state of our society contributes to suffering too. If there were no automobiles, there would be no deaths and injuries resulting from highway accidents. Our air would not be polluted with smoke from factories and automobile exhaust if there were no cars and factories. All of these things are part of the price we pay for our state of civilization. If we do not want to pay the price, we can go back to a more primitive society. In today's world, our lifestyle is a large contributor to sickness and disease.[232]

Of course we can go back to a more primitive society in which factories, automobiles, and other technological threats to our well-being would not exist. The Indians had such an idyllic society before the Pilgrims landed. Of course, we would need to eliminate about 240 million Americans, for the land would be able to feed only about 200,000 of us. But Robertson is right: A return to primitive conditions would probably eliminate highway traffic deaths.

Eliminating several million Americans might not be such a stupid idea after all—at least not when one understands the energy and environmental problems as well as Robertson does:

> The planet does not contain enough nonrenewable and renewable sources of energy to supply indefinitely the basic needs and growing aspirations of a world population that continues to explode.
> It seem's [sic] clear that if we do not make drastic cuts, we face the following perilous prospects. . . .[233]

There then follows a list of evils that we can expect to suffer unless we make "drastic cuts" in our use of fuel. Again, Robertson has not done his homework; indeed, if his method of reading the Bible is any indication, he hasn't the foggiest idea how to do homework. The scare stories of the ecology movement were laid to rest a decade or more ago, and to hear them resurrected by a political candidate who purports to be a Christian and a conservative is a bit startling.

Foreign Policy

Robertson's fatuous domestic policy views are complemented by a messianic vision of American foreign policy. Robertson favors a "New World Order":

Is there truly an invisible world of the spirit?
Is it possible to draw help from that invisible world?
Can there be a new world order?
Yes.[234]

Unfortunately he tells us virtually nothing about this new world order; perhaps a global redistribution of wealth will be one of its characteristics. At another place in his books he makes the following statements: "A new world order is near. It is called the eternal kingdom of heaven, to be brought about by God Almighty. Only certain people will live in it."[235]

But these statements give us little information. I do not know what Robertson means by the phrase "kingdom of God," except that it will be a land of "miracles" and gibberish. Robertson has, however, spoken with more specificity about certain features of present international relations. There will be, if he has his way, an international police force:

> On the international scene, given the sin of mankind, there must be armed forces. Unless there are strong, righteous nations to restrain the adventurism of a Hitler, a Stalin, or a Mao Tse Tung, then all freedoms of all people everywhere will be compromised. There will be nothing but conformity to the will of the dictator, and many innocent people will be killed as that dictator takes power. So it is necessary for the family of nations to raise up an international police force to restrain evil.[236]

In an article in *The Fletcher Forum,* Summer 1987, "Toward a Community of Democratic Nations," Robertson proposes reducing the U.S. contribution to the United Nations by 25 percent and using the money to set up a new "Community of Democratic Nations." This new international organization would be open to "all nations whose governments have achieved legitimacy because they embrace the democratic idea. To qualify for membership, developing states would be required to abandon totalitarianism or dictatorship and to practice democracy for a specified period of time."[237] The CDN would use trade policy, loans, credits, and foreign aid to encourage political freedom in other nations. The CDN could present a "united front against terrorism," and would be able to organize an effective trade embargo against the Soviet Union.

Presumably the "Community of Democratic Nations" is the same as the "family of nations" that forms Robertson's international police force. But neither a Community of Democratic Nations nor an international police force is a new idea. An international police force fought in Korea from 1950 to 1953. The official term for that war was not "war," but "police action." General Douglas MacArthur fought the Communist Koreans and Chinese under the aegis of the United Nations, and his military genius and the blood of thousands of American men were wasted.

Another international police force, also under the aegis of the United Nations, fought in the Congo in the early 1960's, and slaughtered hundreds of innocent people. Still another international police force occupied Beirut in the early 1980s, leading to the violent deaths of hundreds of American soldiers while they slept in their barracks. Robertson endorses this bloody and foolish policy, because he thinks that one of the duties of the United States government is to keep order all over the planet, not to defend the United States. Such a policy of global intervention was not the intention of our Founding Fathers, nor is it compatible with what the Bible says about government.[238] Nevertheless, our government has been pursuing such a messianic foreign policy for the past 75 years with disastrous results: the deaths of millions of people, the rise of Nazism and Communism, the infliction of millions of American casualties, the debasement of our currency, the destruction of public morality, and the squandering of our wealth. Robertson's views promise more blood and more suffering, pursued with an inflamed and messianic zeal, were he to become President.

In order to make clear his intention to continue the messianic foreign policy our government has pursued since World War I, Robertson endorses Woodrow Wilson's goal of making the world safe for democracy.[239] Robertson believes that the federal government ought to have two principles of foreign policy, the first of which is "the defense of the life, liberty, and pursuit of happiness of American citizens." The second principle is "America's commitment to freedom beyond its immediate borders, for its allies and indeed for all people. . . ."[240] In order to save the world, Robertson argues for "much higher quality intelligence gathering operations," "clandestine counter-intelligence infiltrators," and "paramilitary assistance." But on the subject of Nicaragua, he writes: "We don't want a 'dirty little war' in Nicaragua. We want an open drive for freedom."[241] That can only mean war.

Moreover, in order to fight these foreign "police actions," these "open drives for freedom," Robertson would draft Americans: "In time of war, the state has the right to enlist the young for service in the armed forces."[242] But in his newsletter, Robertson does not restrict the draft to times of war:

> The only fair military draft would be some version of universal military training. All youth could be given a choice to serve for a specified period upon graduation from high school or at age 18. All would serve so there would be no discrimination among peers. After a period of active duty some could enlist for longer periods, others could serve short periods of active duty as part of a ready reserve. California congressman Pete McCloskey, a Marine veteran who holds the Navy Cross, has suggested a further option to allow youth civilian government service in lieu of military service.
> Some version of universal military training would be a splendid antidote to juvenile unemployment, delinquency, and the hopelessness of the ghetto.[243]

There are two things that must be noted about these statements: First, Robertson's assertion that the state has the "right" to draft the young; and second, that Robertson's phrases, "the young," and "all youth" seem to imply the drafting of women as well as men.

The Bible and the Draft

The Bible prohibits the drafting of anyone, men or women, into the service of the state. Far from teaching that the state has the right to compel people to serve it, the Bible asserts that the government ought to be the servant of the people.

The first of the many verses that are pertinent to a discussion of the draft is the Eighth Commandment: You shall not steal.[244] This commandment does not refer merely to property, as some have understood: In Exodus 21:16, for example, we read of "manstealing," that is, kidnapping. The Commandment forbids the stealing of both persons and property. The stealing of property is punishable by restitution; the stealing of men, by death.

Nor does this Commandment apply only to individuals; it regulates governments as well. The Ten Commandments bind all men without exception, rulers as well as ruled, governors as well as the governed. King

Ahab stole a vineyard from Naboth—and paid with his life for it.[245] John the Baptist accused Herod of adultery, and he paid with his life for making the accusation.[246] Zacchaeus the tax collector, upon repenting of his sins, offered to repay anything he had taken unjustly from the people.[247]

The Bible furnishes us with specific information about the draft, as well as a general prohibition of it in the Eighth Commandment. In 1 Samuel 8 the history of the origins of the Hebrew monarchy is given: The people demanded a king like all the nations around them.

> But the thing displeased Samuel when they said, "Give us a king to judge us." So Samuel prayed to the Lord.
> And the Lord said to Samuel, "Heed the voice of the people in all that they say to you; for they have not rejected you, but they have rejected Me, that I should not reign over them.... However, you shall solemnly forewarn them, and show them the behavior of the king who will reign over them."
> So Samuel told all the words of the Lord to the people who asked him for a king. And he said, "This will be the behavior of the king who will reign over you: He will take your sons and appoint them for his own chariots and to be his horsemen, and some will run before his chariots. He will appoint captains over his thousands and captains over his fifties, will set some to plow his ground and reap his harvest, and some to make his weapons of war and equipment for his chariots...."

There follows a long list of what the king will take from the people: their sons and daughters; the best of their fields, vineyards, and olive groves; a tenth of their grain, harvests, and wine; their menservants and their maidservants; their finest young men; their donkeys and sheep. God tells Samuel all these things as a warning to the Israelites against the oppression that they will suffer under a king. One of the things explicitly mentioned is a draft: "He will take your sons and appoint them for his own chariots...." God clearly disapproved of a draft, and in the Hebrew Republic—the government that God had established in Israel before the Jews demanded a monarchy—there was no draft.

There is another passage that discusses military service in ancient Israel, Deuteronomy 20:5-8:

> Then the officers shall speak to the people, saying: "What man is

there who has built a new house and has not dedicated it? Let him go and return to his house, lest he die in the battle and another man dedicate it.

"And what man is there who has planted a vineyard and has not yet eaten of it? Let him also go and return to his house, lest he die in the battle and another man eat of it.

"And what man is there who is betrothed to a woman and has not yet married her? Let him go and return to his house, lest he die in the battle and another man marry her.

Then the officers shall speak further to the people, and say, "What man is there who is fearful and fainthearted? Let him go and return to his house, lest the heart of his brethren faint like his heart."

This passage bears a close analysis. Notice that there are four classes of men involved (the references are all to men, none to women, for it was not even contemplated that women would serve in the armed forces of ancient Israel). These four classes of men are prohibited from volunteering for service:

1. Those who have a new house.
2. Those who have a new vineyard.
3. Those who have a fiancee.
4. Those who are afraid.

With regard to the first three classes of men, we are explicitly told by Scripture that their private interests in enjoying their new houses, vineyards, and wives is superior to the national interest in having a larger army in battle. There is no "right" of the state, as Robertson claims, to draft the young into its services. The Bible explicitly says that these domestic pleasures are more important than the national interest. This attitude is even more striking when one recalls that Israel was God's chosen nation, and the wars in which Israel was about to engage were wars specifically commanded by God for the punishment of the idolatrous Canaanite nations. If the private interests of the Hebrew people were more important than the national interest in that situation, how could the national interest of any other nation be superior to private interests today? Today there are no chosen nations. Today there are no divinely commanded wars. Today there is no Promised Land being conquered. If service in ancient Israel's army was voluntary, how much more ought service to be voluntary in the American army?

Let us turn our attention to the fourth and last class of men. First we notice that unlike the men in the first three classes, these men were not sent home because of their private interests, but because their presence in the army would tend to undermine the morale of the troops. Second, the criteria that distinguish the first three classes of men are objective criteria: houses, vineyards, and financees; but the criterion for membership in the last class, the timid, is subjective. Timidity, fearfulness could be determined at the outset by no one except the individual himself. Even assuming that we have totally misunderstood the Eighth Commandment and 1 Samuel 8, this verse alone would make it clear that military service in ancient Israel was voluntary, for the prospective soldier had complete authority to disqualify himself from service. He alone was the judge of whether to fight or not. It also should be noted that he was to go home, if he were fearful. He was not to be forced to perform "alternative service" carrying bedpans or planting trees. In his commentary on this passage the Protestant Reformer John Calvin wrote: "God will not have more required from anyone than he is disposed to bear.... [T]he lazy and timid were sent home, that the Israelites might learn that none were to be pressed beyond their ability; and this also depends upon that rule of equity which dictates that we should abstain from all unjust oppression."

Robertson, of course, has ample precedent for his support of a draft. One of those who thought he might register some people for the draft was David, King of Israel. The account is given in 1 Chronicles 21:

> Satan rose up against Israel and incited David to take a census of Israel.... [B]ut Joab replied [to David], "May the Lord multiply his troops a hundred times over. My lord the king, are they not all my lord's subjects? Why does my lord want to do this? Why should he bring guilt on Israel?... Joab reported the number of the fighting men to David.... But Joab did not include Levi and Benjamin in the numbering, because the king's command was repulsive to him. The command was also evil in the sight of God....

Of course it was evil in the sight of God. This is what Samuel had said in 1 Samuel 8. But Robertson is quite selective in his appeal to the laws of ancient Israel. He endorses the Jubilee law in order to justify a massive redistribution of property in the United States, even though that law was never intended to, and by its content never could, apply to any nation except ancient Israel. But Robertson ignores the Eighth Commandment and the laws governing military service. Such an irrational application of the Bible must be expected from a man who uses his Bible as a Ouija board to get messages from God.

Foreign Aid

Robertson has a most peculiar view of how the Vietnam War should have been handled, or rather avoided. Here are his own words:

> It [Robertson's "law of reciprocity"] is a principle built into the universe. Even international relations respond to it. We Americans saw it at work from the earliest days of the conflict that escalated into the Vietnam War. The escalation was gradual at first. The North Vietnamese and Viet Cong would push at our allies and us. And we would push back, a little harder. They would retaliate, harder, and then back we would come. In such fashion, the United States participated in a dragged-out war that sapped its resources and resolve, simply because of an unwillingness on either side to break the cycle. This should have been done in one of two ways.
> First, we could have loved the enemy and all Southeast Asians, giving them food, clothing, and housing, and doing everything possible to establish them in freedom and the love of God. Love is able to absorb evil actions without fighting back, thus disrupting the cycle of tit for tat. Great faith and courage would have been required while awaiting reciprocal love.
> Second, we could have hit the enemy so fast and so devastatingly as to nullify reciprocal action. Because of the ultimate infallibility of the Law of Reciprocity, however, it seems almost certain that the latter course would have at a point in history, perhaps distant, produced reciprocity from some source.[248]

It is clear that Robertson rejects the second alternative because "the latter course would have at a point in history . . . produced reciprocity," that is, the United States would have been attacked and possibly destroyed, as we had destroyed Vietnam. That leaves only the first alternative: We should have ended the Vietnam War through a massive foreign aid program: "giving them food, clothing, and housing and doing everything possible" for them. Robertson is so much of a busybody in foreign policy that it does not even occur to him that the proper course of action for the United States government was to send neither food nor fighters to North Vietnam, but to mind its own business. Had it done so, it would have saved billions of dollars and tens of thousands of lives.

Dominion Theology

Like many people involved in politics, Robertson tries to find verses in Scripture to support his opinions. One of those verses, commonly misunderstood, is Genesis 1:28: "Then God blessed them, and God said to them, 'Be fruitful and multiply; fill the earth and subdue it; have dominion over the fish of the sea, over the birds of the air, and over every living thing that moves on the earth.'"

The verse clearly gives mankind dominion over the animals and the earth. It does not give men dominion over men. Yet Robertson's misunderstanding of the verse is today a very common one: "God's plan, ladies and gentlemen, is for his people to take dominion.... What is dominion? Dominion is Lordship. He wants His people to reign and rule with him."[249] In Robertson's view, while dominion includes such things as agriculture and technology, it also includes the much more important function of political rule. This is the explanation for his "international police force," his government regulation of the economy, and his campaign for President itself. By running for office, he sees himself as exercising dominion.

It is precisely this sort of political dominion that is forbidden to Christians by Christ himself:

> But Jesus called them [his disciples] unto him, and said, "You know that the princes of the Gentiles exercise dominion over them, and they that are great exercise authority upon them. But it shall not be so among you; but whoever will be great among you, let him be your minister [servant]. And whosoever will be chief among you, let him be your servant: even as the Son of Man came not to be ministered unto, but to minister, and to give His life a ransom for many."[250]

This passage is the origin of the idea that the purpose of government is to be a servant of the people, not their master, an idea that was to become very influential in American history. Dominion theology, which depends on confusing dominion over animals with dominion over men, is an error at the foundation of Robertson's political theory and a blunder of the first order.[251] Any man running for office who states, as Robertson does, that he wants to exercise dominion over men, is acting contrary to what Christ himself commanded.

Public Education

One of the legitimate functions of government, according to Robertson, is the operation of public schools: "The state has a stake in general literacy, so it can establish educational standards, public schools, and truancy laws."[252] By the same bizarre "logic," since the state has a stake in general health, it can establish health standards, erect state cafeterias, and compel attendance at them. Robertson's argument, even assuming his premise that the state has a legitimate interest in literacy, is fallacious. It is not surprising, then, that his conclusion finds no support in the Bible either.

Robertson's views on education seem a little incoherent. He has written,

> Since the government should be neutral as to religion, and since education by its very nature must have a moral framework, why not get government entirely out of education? Let the churches, private academies, and educational societies take over elementary education entirely. The states could assess and accredit the institutions of learning as to core curriculum and teacher credentials, without reference to theistic preference or lack of it.[253]

But a close reading of this longer explanation of his views indicates that Robertson believes government should retain the power to regulate all schools, and that such private schools as are permitted to exist would offer only elementary education.

According to the Bible, education is a duty of parents, not governors. Paul outlines the duties of rulers in Romans 13:

> Let every soul be subject to the governing authorities. For there is no authority except from God, and the authorities that exist are appointed by God. Therefore whoever resists the authority resists the ordinance of God, and those who resist will bring judgment on themselves. For rulers are not a terror to good works, but to evil.

> Do you want to be unafraid of the authority? Do what is good, and you will have praise from the same. For he is God's minister to you for good. But if you do evil be afraid; for he does not bear the sword in vain; for he is God's minister, an avenger to execute wrath on him who practices evil.

The purpose of government is to punish evildoers. The ruler bears the sword of capital punishment and war. It is not the function of rulers to educate the populace, but to see that justice is done and evildoers are punished. Education is a function of the parents and their schools:

> And these words which I command you today shall be in your heart; and you shall teach them diligently to your children, and shall talk of them when you sit in your house, when you walk by the way, when you lie down, and when you rise up.[254] And you, fathers, do not provoke your children to wrath, but bring them up in the training and admonition of the Lord.[255]

To say that the government "can establish educational standards, public schools and truancy laws" contradicts everything the Bible says about the proper functions of governments and parents.

Conclusion

Pat Robertson's political views, even though many of his supporters are conservatives, are not all conservative. He favors the repudiation of the national debt, the cancellation of all private debt, the periodic redistribution of "all accumulated property," the formation of an international police force, massive foreign aid, government control of education, and a military draft. Why, then, do conservatives support him? They apparently see him as a very religious man, and being generally religious themselves, they think that religion is a good thing. It is not. Christianity is a good thing, and Christianity is primarily a critique of all religions. Religion is a tool of diabolic powers, powers who have persuaded most of the people on this planet to hate Christianity with a religious and pious passion. There is no value in being religious. Only truth is valuable, and, as we have seen, Pat Robertson has difficulty determining what the truth is. In the next chapter we will explain why.

Chapter 7
Beyond Reason

Come, let us reason together, says the Lord.

Isaiah 18:1.

Pat Robertson's race for the Presidency was made possible by three European thinkers who lived nearly two centuries ago: Immanuel Kant, the German philosopher, Soren Kierkegaard, the Danish philosopher, and Friedrich Schleiermacher, the German theologian. The names are unfamiliar to most Americans, but their ideas are not. These three thinkers and their disciples have shaped the reigning philosophies of the world.

From Kant, the world learned that reality is deeper than logic; there are things that can be known, and things that are unknowable. Kant called one of these unknowable things "God." From the Great Dane, the world learned that truth is subjective, not objective; that paradoxes and contradictions, not consistency, are the mark of truth. From Schleiermacher, the world learned that the essence of religion is feeling, specifically a feeling of absolute dependence.

All three men, enormously brilliant and enormously influential, were anti-intellectuals. Kant wrote complex *Critiques* of pure and practical reason. Kierkegaard said, "It was intelligence and nothing else that had to be opposed. Presumably that is why I, who had the job, was armed with an immense intelligence."[256] Schleiermacher added, "All true human feelings belong to the religious sphere, all ideas and principles of every sort are foreign to it."[257]

In the last third of the eighteenth century secular philosophers launched a frenetic and strident attack on logic. Theologians soon joined the attack, an assault that has now been sustained for two centuries. Immanuel Kant, Soren Kierkegaard, Friedrich Schleiermacher, Friedrich Nietzsche, Karl Marx, and the Romantic movement were early aggressors; in this century they have been reinforced by the pragmatists, the existentialists, the positivists, the behaviorists, the neo-orthodox, and the liberals. Pat Robertson is their spiritual heir.

Mindless Religion

We have already commented on Robertson's mindless way of reading the Bible: letting it fall open, stabbing at the page with his finger, and then interpreting whatever sentence he points to as referring to himself. But the irrationality of his position goes much deeper than that. His basic irrationalism is the explanation for his enthusiasm about experience. The movement which he represents long ago declared war on rational thought, and, thereby, on Christianity. Christianity is first and foremost a revelation from the rational God. The revelation is given in words and propositions. Christians are commanded to study the Bible until they understand it.

But the Charismatic movement will have none of this. One of the original best selling books by a Charismatic was *They Speak With Other Tongues,* by John L. Sherrill, an editor of Norman Vincent Peale's *Guideposts* magazine. Sherrill opens his book by recounting a sermon that "was to hold the key to the most astonishing experience of my life."

> At the time it seemed wretchedly irrelevant to my problem. The young man gave a short talk on Nicodemus. "Many of us try," he said, "to approach Christ as Nicodemus did: through logic. . . .
>
> "But, you see," said the seminarian, "as long as Nicodemus was trying to come to an understanding of Christ through his logic, he could never succeed. It isn't logic, but an experience, that lets us know who Christ is."[258]

Soon after that sermon, Catherine Marshall, widow of the chaplain of the U.S. Senate, Peter Marshall, told Sherrill: "You're trying to approach Christianity through your mind, John. It simply can't be done that way. . . You cannot come to it through intellect. You have to be willing to experience it first. . . ."[259]

One of the most recent best selling Charismatic books, *Power Evangelism* by John Wimber, makes this statement: "First century Semites did not argue from a premise to a conclusion; they were not controlled by rationalism."[260] Now Christ was certainly a first century Semite. He was, in fact, *the* first century Semite. Did he argue from premise to conclusion?

Christ and Logic

The New Testament is replete with examples of how Paul, the other apostles, and Christ himself argued logically. Take for example, Christ's reply to the argument of the Sadducees that there is no resurrection:

> The same day the Sadducees, who say there is no resurrection, came to Him and asked Him, saying: 'Teacher, Moses said that if a man dies, having no children, his brother shall marry his wife and raise up offspring for his brother. Now there were with us seven brothers. The first died after he had married, and having no offspring, left his wife to his brother. Likewise the second also, and the third, even to the seventh. And last of all the woman died also. Therefore, in the resurrection, whose wife of the seven will she be? For they all had her."[261]

The Sadducees obviously thought that this was a conclusive argument against the resurrection. Let us pay attention then to what Christ says in reply:

> Jesus answered and said to them, "You are mistaken, not knowing the Scriptures nor the power of God. For in the resurrection they neither marry nor are given in marriage, but are like angels of God in heaven. But concerning the resurrection of the dead, have you not read what was spoken to you by God, saying, 'I am the God of Abraham, the God of Isaac, and the God of Jacob'? God is not the God of the dead but of the living."[262]

Notice exactly what Christ does. Unlike the Charismatics, he does not attack the Sadducees for using "mere human logic." He does not attack them for having too much head knowledge. He does precisely the opposite. He attacks these learned men for their ignorance of Scripture and their mistakes in logic: "You are mistaken, not knowing the

Scriptures nor the power of God." Christ criticized Nicodemus for the same reason: his ignorance: "Are you the teacher of Israel and do not know these things?"[263]

Christ replies to the argument of the Sadducees by first correcting their ignorance of the state of the elect in heaven: They neither marry nor are given in marriage. By saying this, Christ destroys this particular argument of the Sadducees, for it was upon the logical impossibility of deciding whose wife this woman was that they concluded that there could be no resurrection. Their argument is that the hypothesis of the resurrection, plus the eternity of marriage, leads to an absurd conclusion, one woman with seven husbands. Christ demolishes their argument by replying that marriage is dissolved by death, just as Paul emphasizes in Romans 7. Indeed, the Sadducees should have deduced this from the fact that the woman's seven marriages were all legal: Each prior marriage had been dissolved by the death of her husband. Therefore, the dead and resurrected woman is nobody's wife. Obviously, if there is no marriage in heaven, then the Sadducees' argument collapses. The absurdity that they perceived did not stem from the notion of a resurrection, but from their erroneous notion of the eternity of marriage.

So much for stage one of Christ's reply. He has shown that this specific argument from marriage does not refute the resurrection. But more is needed to refute the Sadducees thoroughly. While Christ has destroyed this particular argument, perhaps the Sadducees had others that they would bring up later. So Christ goes further: He deduces the resurrection from two Old Testament propositions: God is not the God of the dead, but of the living; and, God is the God of Abraham, Isaac, and Jacob. Therefore, Abraham, Isaac, and Jacob are not dead but living. Death is not the end; there is a resurrection. The conclusion is deduced by good and necessary consequence from the premises. Now the Sadducees have no place to escape. Not only has their marriage argument collapsed, but their general position has been refuted by logical deductions from Scripture. Christ is more than a little sarcastic when he asks these men who were supposed to be the teachers of Israel: "Have you not read what was spoken to you by God?"

In this example we have a model of Christian power evangelism, as opposed to fraudulent Charismatic power evangelism. First, Christ tells the Sadducees that they are wrong: You are mistaken. Then he tells them why: You do not know the Scriptures nor the power of God which is capable of raising people from the dead. Third: He refutes their specific argument. Fourth: He refutes their general position by making logical deductions from Scripture. Is it any wonder, when Christ had finished his thoroughly logical refutation of the Sadducees, that the multitudes "were astonished at his teaching"?[264]

The multitudes then may have been astonished at Christ's teaching, but some Charismatic leaders today, like some religious leaders of Christ's day, would be very angry. They maintain that human logic is not to be trusted. Wimber writes that "There was a mistrust [among first century Semites for] . . . theological truths through abstract reasoning."[265] So if all dogs have teeth, and Pit Bulls are dogs, then Pit Bulls do not have teeth. But of course this is a "canine truth," rather than a theological truth. Well, if God is the God of the living, and also the God of Abraham, Isaac and Jacob, then there is no resurrection, and the Sadducees were right. That seems sufficiently theological. It is also thoroughly Wimberian. What it is not, is Christian. Christ, unlike John Wimber and the Charismatics, used "human logic" to defend the faith. Any religion that cannot accept Christ's use of logic is not Christianity.

The anti-logic and anti-intellectual views of the Charismatics are certainly not Biblical, and they are irreconcilable with Christian theology. Let me quote from Princeton Seminary Professor Benjamin Warfield's book, *The Westminster Assembly and Its Work*, on this point:

> It must be observed, however, that the teachings and prescriptions of Scripture are not confined by the [Westminster] Confession to what is "expressly set down in Scripture." Men are required to believe and to obey not only what is "expressly set down in Scripture," but also what "by good and necessary consequence may be deduced from Scripture."

If I may add an aside here, this contention is fully supported by the example I have cited. Christ reproached the Sadducees for not believing what could have been and what should have been deduced by good and necessary consequence from the Old Testament. To go on with Warfield:

> This is the strenuous and universal contention of the Reformed theology against Socinians and Arminians, who desired to confine the authority of Scripture to its literal asseverations; and it involves a characteristic

honoring of reason as the instrument for the ascertainment of truth. We must depend upon our human faculties to ascertain what Scripture says, we cannot suddenly abnegate them and refuse their guidance in determining what Scripture means. This is not, of course, to make reason the ground of the authority of inferred doctrines and duties. Reason is the instrument of discovery of all doctrines and duties, whether "expressly set down in Scripture" or "by good and necessary consequence deduced from Scripture": but their authority, when once discovered, is derived from God, who reveals and prescribes them in Scripture, either by literal assertion or by necessary implication.... It is the Reformed contention, reflected here by the Confession, that the sense of Scripture is Scripture, and that men are bound by its whole sense in all its implications. The re-emergence in recent controversies of the plea that the authority of Scripture is to be confined to its expressed declarations, and that human logic is not to be trusted in divine things, is, therefore, a direct denial of a fundamental position of Reformed theology, explicitly affirmed in the Confession, as well as an abnegation of fundamental reason, which would not only render thinking in a system impossible, but would discredit at a stroke many of the fundamentals of the faith, such e.g. as the doctrine of the Trinity, and would logically involve the denial of the authority of all doctrine whatsoever, since no single doctrine of whatever simplicity can be ascertained from Scripture except by use of the processes of the understanding.... The recent plea against the use of human logic in determining doctrine ... destroys at once our confidence in all doctrines, no one of which is ascertained or formulated without the aid of human logic.[266]

Thus the anti-logic position of the Charismatics is not new at all; it has been used by many heretical movements. They all are mistaken, not knowing the Scriptures nor the power of God.

More Examples

Perhaps there is someone who thinks at this point that Christ's argument with the Sadducees is the only such argument to be found in Scripture. He might wish to turn to 1 Corinthians 15 and read Paul's chapter on the Gospel. Let me assure the reader that all Scriptural arguments can be put into logical form, some more easily than others. Here are a few of the more obvious examples:

John 8:47: "He who is of God hears God's words; therefore you do not hear, because you are not of God."

If *p*, then *q*; not *q*, therefore not *p*.

John 18:36: "My kingdom is not of this world. If my kingdom were of this world, my servants would fight, so that I should not be delivered to the Jews; but now my kingdom is not from here."

If my kingdom were of this world, my servants would fight. My servants do not fight, therefore my kingdom is not of this world.

If *p*, then *q*; not *q*, therefore not *p*.

John 9:41: "If you were blind, you would have no sin; but now you say, 'We see.' Therefore your sins remains."

This verse is an excellent example of an *ad hominem* argument, which is not to be confused with the logical fallacy of the same name. In such an argument, one assumes, for the sake of argument, the position of one's opponent. That is precisely what Christ does here. He is teaching that responsibility is based on knowledge: If you were ignorant, you would have no sin. But since the Pharisees did not claim to be ignorant, but to know, then they were sinful. Their very claim to know made them responsible.

Another example of Christ using an *ad hominem* argument is found in Matthew 12:11-12: "What man is there among you who has one sheep, and if it falls into a pit on the Sabbath, will not lay hold of it and lift it out? Of how much more value then is a man than a sheep? Therefore it is lawful to do good on the Sabbath."

The Pharisees were trying to trap Jesus by asking him whether it is lawful to heal on the Sabbath. Jesus takes two premises, both of which the Pharisees would agree with, (1) that it is lawful to rescue a sheep in distress on the Sabbath, and (2) that a man is more valuable than a sheep; and He deduces from them that it is lawful to rescue a man in distress on the Sabbath. From their own views Christ deduces the lawfulness of the action that they believed was unlawful, and thus He refutes them. What can those who hate logic do with a man who is so adept at using logic? Only what the Pharisees did: "Then the Pharisees went out and took counsel against Him, how they might destroy him."[267]

Later in the same chapter Christ sets up a complex argument in order to refute the Pharisees. The first part of this argument is a complex syllogism in which the conclusion is stated as a rhetorical question: "Every kingdom divided against itself is brought to desolation, and every city or house divided against itself will not stand. And if Satan casts out

Satan, he is divided against himself. How then will his kingdom stand?"[268]

The situation, as you recall, is the accusation of the Pharisees that Christ was casting out demons by the power of Beelzebub, the ruler of demons. Jesus refutes the accusation:

All divided kingdoms cannot stand.
If Satan casts out Satan, his kingdom is divided.
Therefore his kingdom cannot stand.

Christ does not let the matter drop there. He has already demonstrated that by the Pharisees' own assumption, Satan's kingdom is being destroyed by Christ. But He goes on to drive the point home again, a practice that Christian evangelists ought to imitate. It is not enough to demonstrate the logical absurdity of an attack on Christianity once or in only one way. It ought to be done repeatedly and in as many ways as possible. Christ engages in what delicate and squeamish people call overkill. He continues: "And if I cast out demons by Beelzebub, by whom do your sons cast them out? Therefore they shall be your judges. But if I cast out demons by the Spirit of God, surely the kingdom of God has come upon you."

Let's take a moment and unpack this dilemma. Christ is arguing that if He is casting out demons by the power of the Devil, then so were the sons of the Pharisees, the young Jewish men—perhaps the 70 of Luke 10—that He had given power over the demons. Is that what the Pharisees believed? He was forcing them to understand one of the implications of their accusation. If Christ was an agent of Beelzebub, then so were the sons of the Pharisees, who were also casting out demons using the power that Christ had given them. And if the sons of the Pharisees were agents of Satan, then they would be a judgment to their fathers.

On the other hand, if Christ was who He said He was, then the kingdom of God has come, which the Pharisees vigorously denied. Either way, Christ argues, you lose. You will be judged for your unbelief.

Irrationalism and the Demonic

There are many more Scriptural examples of the sort of logical argument that the Charismatics dislike. Anyone who belittles the usefulness or the lawfulness of logic is simply showing his ignorance or unbelief of Scripture. Unfortunately, many Charismatics do so. Consider these statements from leading Charismatics:

> This phenomena [sic, of speaking in tongues] necessarily violates human reason. It means abandonment of this faculty for the time. And this is generally the last point to yield. The human mind is held in abeyance fully in this exercise.[269]
>
> Another big factor has been the tremendous emphasis in Western Christendom on the mind and human reason—leaving little or no room for more direct inspiration. If it is thought that the mind has a monopoly in the realm of edification, then there is obviously no room for the gift of tongues. . . .[270]

A most striking instance of the danger posed by such mindlessness is this testimony from a former missionary in China, who attended a Charismatic meeting:

> However, when one of my missionary associates standing beside me suddenly became agitated and began shouting loudly in excellent Chinese, leaping and waving his arms and obviously under the control of a power quite beyond himself, my resistance weakened. I didn't want to be left out of the blessing that he was receiving. I let my mind become quite blank and began yielding myself to the external power outside myself that seemed to be pleading for full control of me.
> At once a feeling of paralysis began to numb my feet. It soon affected my legs. I knew that before long I too would be lying helplessly on the floor as were several others in the crowd. At the instant the numbness reached my knees, I became alarmed. "This thing is coming upon me, not from heaven, but from beneath. This is the wrong direction," I thought to myself. Without a moment's hesitation, I cried out, "May the blood of Christ protect me from this thing!" At once it vanished and I was normal again.
> A month later I met that co-worker of mine at another place. He appeared to be a sober and chastened man. "You know, Ray, that thing that happened to me that night wasn't of God. It was of the devil." . . . [M]y friend then described the spiritual darkness into which he was plunged, following that ecstatic experience.[271]

Once one has abandoned the completed revelation of the Bible, once one has let his mind become quite blank, once one has given oneself over—in religious terms, yielded or surrendered to—the powers that want to control you, then one is deeply into demonism. That is the result of moving, as Robertson recommends, Beyond Reason.

Chapter 8
President Robertson?

A bottomless pit of fanaticism is yawning.
Charles Haddon Spurgeon

Pat Robertson has been misleading people for decades. He himself confesses to several instances of deception—perhaps not deliberate—in his books. Moreover, he has been deceived on many occasions. He has been approached by "angels of Light," he has heard voices, and he has felt impressions that misled him. He has made predictions that failed and announced miracles that he could not produce. His entire adult life has been the practice of religious deception—claiming to hear God's voice, to speak for God, to perform divine miracles.

In one of his books Robertson defines lying as follows:

> Lying is a deliberate attempt to deceive by the use of any form of untruth. By words, gestures, circumstances, or silence an attempt may be made to convince another that there is a reality different from what we know to be true...
>
> A person who falsifies his achievements or age is lying. A person who covers up or exaggerates facts is lying.[272]

Judged by his own definition, Robertson has been lying since his Presidential ambitions became publicly known. He has exaggerated his military service in Korea; he has lied about the date of his marriage; and he has embellished his academic studies at the University of London in

1950. These deceptions by themselves are hardly worth mentioning. But they are a part of a much larger pattern of deception that seems to have begun even before he had his first religious experience in 1956. Even before Robertson "had a personal experience with Jesus Christ," he heard God telling him that he ought to be a minister:

> Another of those strange feelings that had been clouding up my thoughts with increasing frequency for the past year settled over me. *God has a purpose for your life.* An inaudible voice seemed to be speaking in the deep recesses of my mind.
> God.[273]

Now it may be that Pat Robertson truly believes what he says, at least part of the time. It is also true that the most deceiving people are those who are sincerely deceived. But whatever the state of his mind, for the past thirty years Robertson has been acting out a colossal deception, a deception so large that it has already impugned Christianity and now threatens the United States with political calamity.

Robertson is a representative, a leader, of what has been called the "Third Force" in Christendom. The Charismatic movement is not totally new; there have been eruptions of fanaticism in earlier centuries, but few so large and so powerful as those in this century. No earlier fanatic had control of a network of radio and television stations, no holy roller had access to satellite technology. No whirling dervish had hundreds of thousands of campaign contributors. The tools that Robertson has at his disposal, tools which he has shown himself capable of using very effectively, have attracted millions of people to his message of experiential religion and politics.

Former Senator Paul Laxalt, reportedly one of Ronald Reagan's best friends, quit the race for the Presidency because he could not raise two million dollars. Robertson has already raised and spent more than $11 million. The Republican National Committee has about 8,000 donors in New Hampshire, the first primary state. Robertson's CBN has 50,000. Robertson attracts dedicated followers and campaign workers, many more than the other Republican contenders. His political strategists and paid field staff know how to win, and they showed their clout early in Michigan, Iowa, and Florida.

If Robertson is successful in his campaign for the Presidency, he may very well lead America into war abroad and economic catastrophe at home. His views on foreign policy and domestic affairs, views which he falsely believes to be sanctioned by God, will, if executed, cause a catastrophe for America unlike anything she has yet experienced. It will prove difficult, if not impossible, to dissuade Robertson from any course of action he decides to take once the voices which drive him tell him what to do. There is no discussion possible, no persuasion feasible, with a man who is certain that he is listening to the voice of God.

There is an old Roman proverb which says, Whom the gods wish to destroy, they first make mad. That is pretty good theology, but it becomes much better and completely true if we state it monotheistically: Whom God wishes to destroy, He first makes mad. The movement that Robertson represents is a movement of religious madness. If he, or it, is successful in the pursuit of power, America may never recover.

Postscript

The Origin and Destiny of the Charismatic Movement[274]

The sixteenth century rediscovery of the Bible's objective message of justification by faith alone invaded the consciousness of men with divine power and changed the course of history. The Protestant movement was founded upon a restoration of the primacy, supremacy, and all-sufficiency of the Bible and justification by faith.

No one would want to contend that the Protestant Reformation completely recovered the purity of the faith and practice which existed in the apostolic church. The Reformers did not always agree among themselves. They were not always consistent in every area. The church did not all at once abandon every error of the Dark Ages. But in spite of differences and inconsistencies, the Reformers were absolutely united on the primacy of Scripture and the centrality of justification by faith alone.

There is a tendency in sinful human nature to gravitate from the objective gospel to religious subjectivism, to shift the central focus from Christ to Christian experience. This is what happened in the great "falling away" in the early church. And the same evolution has taken place within the Protestant movement.

The Error of the Sects

Even before the Reformers had passed off the stage, different sects began to grow up within the Protestant movement and to break from the founding churches. The sects said that Luther made a good start in reviving the doctrine of justification by faith alone, but they had the feeling that Luther stopped only half way and that they must go on, higher up and deeper in.

But Luther discerned that they erred on the great charter of Protestantism—justification by faith alone—and, as far as he was concerned, if this was wrong, everything was wrong. "Whoever departs from the article of justification does not know God and is an idolator," wrote Luther. "For when this article has been taken away, nothing remains but error, hypocrisy, godlessness, and idolatry, although it may seem to be the height of truth, worship of God, holiness, etc."[275]

These sectarian teachers did not deny justification as an initiating step in the Christian life. Their error was the old one of relegating justification to something whereby the believer can make a start and then go on to higher things. With them, justification by faith was no longer the center. Their focus was away from Christ's work to their own, from the objective to the subjective.

In the time of the Reformers, the Munzerites and radical Anabaptists gave great prominence to the work and gifts of the Spirit. Their cry was, "The Spirit! The Spirit!" but Luther replied, "I will not follow where their spirit leads." They were the sixteenth century Charismatics.

Then there was Andreas Osiander (1498-1552). At first a disciple and co-laborer with Luther, he broke from the Reformation teaching on justification by an imputed righteousness and began to teach that the believer is justified by the indwelling of Christ and His essential righteousness. Both Luther and Calvin recognized that Osiander's teaching was a return, in principle, to the Roman Catholic idea of justification. Some of the sects erred from the Gospel in that they tried to go beyond righteousness by faith to seeking a state of absolute sinlessness in this mortal life on earth. The Reformers also recognized that this was actually Roman Catholic perfectionism in new garments.

After the time of the Reformers, the Protestant movement went through a period known as Protestant orthodoxy, during which heresies were resisted by a careful definition of the Christian faith. The rediscoveries of the Gospel and the whole counsel of God made during the Reformation were organized and codified in various creeds and confessions, the most remarkable of which is the *Westminster Confession of Faith*. But in Germany, Pietism arose as a reaction against the hypocrisy of the state-sanctioned Lutheran church. Misunderstanding the reason for the lifelessness of the Lutheran church, the Pietists thought it was a lack of "experimental religion," rather than simply unbelief and hypocrisy. The tendency of Pietism was to distort the objective Gospel with an exaggerated emphasis on experience. Much of the German Pietism captured the spirit of the Roman Catholic mystics and resembled it in its sentimental and effeminate Christian devotions.

Wesleyanism

Eighteenth century England witnessed a remarkable movement which was also a reaction to the formalism of the state Church of England. The truth of justification by faith had been largely lost from the church. Those were the days of the foxhunting parsons who loved their dogs more than the flock. Moreover, there was a growing working class, unchurched and untouched by an indifferent church. John Wesley (1703-1791) was an outstanding man of the eighteenth century. His effect on the national life of England (especially on the working class) was so remarkable that some credit his ministry, together with that of George Whitefield (1714-1770), with saving England from a revolution similar to that which engulfed France in 1789.

John Wesley believed in justification by faith. His long suit, however, was sanctification. He had been deeply influenced by Moravian Pietism and certain of the Roman Catholic mystics. But Wesley's emphasis on sanctification was the weakness of the Methodist movement. Along with justification by the blood of Christ, Wesley emphasized the renewing power of the Holy Spirit in conforming lives to true obedience to the law of God. Apart from sanctified obedience to the law of God, Wesley declared that no soul would retain the blessing of justification.

Because of his Arminianism, with its denial of the complete depravity of the human heart and its assertion of free will, Wesley developed a doctrine of entire sanctification, known also as the "second blessing" or "Methodist perfection." He proposed that after justification and a process of sanctification, the believer would receive by faith a sudden second blessing which would completely purge the soul of inbred sin, enabling the fully sanctified soul to feel nothing but perfect love. He called this experience "a still higher salvation," "immensely greater than that wrought when he was justified."[276] Wesley and his preachers urged their hearers to seek this second blessing of perfection with all diligence. They did, and gave proof of it in lives of earnest (and sometimes frantic) piety.

With Paul and Luther, the objective work of Jesus Christ in the atonement and the objective work of God the Father in justification by faith was the whole truth of the Gospel. But in Wesleyanism, the effects of the Gospel became more important than the Gospel itself. The centrality of justification tended to be lost by being subordinated to sanctification.

However, it must be said to Wesley's credit that, although he preached entire perfection and the second blessing to others, until his dying day he frankly confessed that he had not attained it. He always sought it, but attained only the hope of it. He was too humble and honest to confess anything but that he still felt sin strong within him—although few men exhibited a mastery over inbred sin as well as he did.

Unfortunately, not all of Wesley's followers were as prudent or as humble as he was. The trouble deepened when some of them professed that they had attained the second blessing of entire sanctification. A few were preachers, and some of these soon fell to the temptation of imagining that they were superior to Wesley. The Methodist revival was therefore plagued and embarrassed by fanaticism. The problem did not come to the surface as long as all the Methodists were seeking perfection. It boiled over when some claimed to have attained it.

This also must be said in Wesley's favor. Most of his labors were directed toward preaching the Gospel to the unsaved, although his gospel was different from the Gospel of Paul and Luther. But he was obliged to spend most of his time preaching justification by faith to sinners. This was a great providential blessing, for it kept the evangelist in better balance. The same thing cannot be said for all of Wesley's spiritual children.

American Revivalism and the Holiness Movement

In the seventeenth and eighteenth centuries, Calvinism was the dominant theology of America. But late eighteenth and nineteenth century American Protestantism became heir to much of Methodism's religious fervor. America developed its own style and brand of revivalism. It suited the national temper and was molded by the frontier spirit.

Frontier life was rude, raw, and exciting. Some of the frontier people saw very little of churches or preachers except once a year at a big tent revival meeting. As the growing calves were rounded up once a year for branding, so the growing youth needed to be gathered in and "saved," while the older people felt their need for a good "clean-up" in the yearly revival time. Revivals, of course, were demanded by the Arminian and Wesleyan theology that taught that one could lose one's salvation by sinning. Vinson Synan has well said, "Those who attended such camp meetings... generally expected their religious experiences to be as vivid as the frontier life around them. Accustomed to 'braining bears and battling Indians,' they received their religion with great color and excitement."[277]

Sometimes the religious fervor was accompanied by great emotional excesses such as "godly hysteria," falling, jerking, "the holy laugh," barking like dogs, and "such wild dances as David performed before the Ark of the Lord."

Charles Finney was such a successful evangelist that, by 1850, revivalism—Charles Finney style—became almost the national religion of America. Finney's systematic theology (which is still one of the most popular manuals on theology in the Pentecostal and Charismatic churches today) is very critical of Luther and Calvin with respect to their teaching of justification by faith through the imputed righteousness of Christ. Finney's predominant emphasis was on sanctification and God's work within human experience—an emphasis which is neither Biblical nor Reformational. His preaching led people into a very emotional experience and seeking after a holiness of experience that would be acceptable to God.

In all these revival influences, the predominant emphasis was to "find God" in a very dramatic, emotional, inward experience of the "heart." There was very little attention given to being declared acceptable to God through faith in a righteousness not our own but wholly outside of us in the person of Christ. American revivalism was far more subjective than objective, far more experience-centered than Gospel-centered.

About the middle of the nineteenth century, the Methodist Church (which was then the largest church in the United States) experienced a remarkable resurgence of interest in the doctrine of the "second blessing." The decade of the 1840s witnessed a flood of perfectionistic teaching in the Methodist church. Leading pastors, bishops, and theologians led the movement, giving it institutional and intellectual respectability.

This development spilled over into other Protestant bodies, and by 1869 it became known as the "holiness movement." Independent "holiness" publications sprang up all over the country. The movement spread to England and found expression in the famous Keswick Convention.

The idea popularized in the holiness movement was the victorious Spirit-filled life. Its focal point was not on justification or even conversion but on the attainment of an experience of holiness and entire sanctification subsequent to conversion. George Dana Boardman (1828-1903), A.B. Simpson (1844-1919), founder of the Christian and Missionary Alliance church, R.A. Torrey (1865-1928), associate of Dwight L. Moody (1837-1899) and head of the Moody Bible Institute, and Andrew Murray (1828-1917) were some of the best-known writers and leaders of the movement. Hannah Whitall Smith's *The Christian's Secret of a Happy Life* (still in print and widely circulated today) expressed very well the aspirations of the holiness people. Holiness-type books can generally be detected by titles that major on experience rather than on the Gospel or doctrines: *The Victorious Life, Keys to Victorious Living, The Spirit-Filled Life*, etc. The punch line of these books is generally on Romans 7 and Romans 8: "Get out of Romans 7 and into Romans 8" (which, incidentally, is contrary to what the Reformers all taught).

The objective nature and value of justification and forgiveness ceased to be the center of the teaching of the holiness movement. They were undervalued, demeaned, and belittled in the overwhelming preoccupation with religious experience and perfectionism. The holiness movement ran aground on the rocks of subjectivism, and because of this, it is more in harmony with Roman Catholicism than with the teaching of the Bible.

In the 1890s the Methodist church took an administrative stand against the holiness movement. Consequently, between the years 1890 and 1900, twenty-three holiness denominations were formed.

The Pentecostal Movement

Toward the end of the nineteenth century, many within the holiness movement began to speak about and seek for the "baptism of fire." One branch of the holiness movement was called the "Fire-Baptized Holiness Church" originating in Iowa in 1895 and led by Benjamin Irwin. Those receiving "the fire" would often shout, scream, fall into trances or speak gibberish. This "baptism of fire" was regarded as a miraculous visitation of the Spirit that followed entire sanctification. The more conservative teachers of the holiness movement rejected this "third" blessing of fire, for they regarded the second blessing and the special baptism of the Spirit as synonymous.

But the radical "fire" advocates continued to make an impact within the movement with fiery preaching and publications like *Live Coals Of Fire* (first published in October 1899). This paper spoke of "the blood that cleans up, the Holy Ghost that fills up, the fire that burns up, and the dynamite that blows up." It is not hard to imagine the eccentric and mind-bending manifestations that accompanied the blowing-up stage of this religious high. The logical outcome of this religious trend was the appearance of the twentieth century Pentecostal movement, which generally traces its beginnings to the ministry of Charles Parham, a Methodist preacher, in Topeka, Kansas in 1900.

Frederick Dale Bruner wrote, "Out of the world-wide holiness movements the Pentecostal movement was born. The Pentecostal historian, Charles Conn, notes that 'the Pentecostal movement is an extension of the holiness revival that occurred during the last half of the nineteenth century.' "[278]

Says noted Roman Catholic author and advocate of church unification, Kilian McDonnell, "John Wesley was father to much of the 19th century American religious fervor; one of his children was the Holiness Movement which gave rise to the Pentecostalism of the 20th century."[279]

The Pentecostal movement came into being directly on the issue of insisting that the physical sign of speaking in "tongues" was the evidence of the baptism of the Spirit. This issue of tongues caused a split between the holiness and Pentecostal movements; yet the basic theology of the two movements remained the same.

Pentecostalism is the inevitable outcome of subjective revivalism. It is American revivalism in its penultimate form of development. The kind of revivals that operate in the United States may not be overtly Pentecostal or Charismatic, but they tend in that direction because they are supremely oriented toward religious experientialism.

The Trend Toward Rome

For more than four hundred years influences have been at work within the Protestant movement to erode the objective emphasis of the Reformation doctrine of justification by faith. There has been a drift back to Romanism. A few years ago, the noted Roman Catholic author, Louis Bouyer, made this stunning observation:

> The Protestant revival . . . recalls the best and most authentic elements of the Catholic tradition. . . . We see in every Protestant country, Christians who owed their religion to the movement we have called, in general, revivalism, attain a more or less complete discovery of Catholicism. . . .
> The contemporary revivals most valuable and lasting in their results all present a striking analogy with this process of rediscovery of Catholicism. . . . [T]he instinctive orientation of the revivals toward the Catholic . . . would bring in that way a reconciliation between the Protestant Movement and the Church. . . .[280]

Bouyer closes with an appeal to his fellow Catholics to prepare for the inevitable return of the "separated brethren" under the influence of contemporary revivals. The fact that some revivalists regard themselves as anti-Catholic makes no difference, for, as Bouyer points out, they are simply in the dark about how their theology is in profound harmony with Catholicism.

A few years ago, liberal theologian Paul Tillich observed that we have reached "the end of the Protestant era."

> For the kind of Protestantism which has developed in America is not so much an expression of the Reformation, but has more to do with the so-called Evangelical Radicals. There are the Lutheran and Calvinistic groups, and they are strong, but they have adapted themselves to an astonishing degree to the climate of American Protestantism. This climate

has not been made by them, but by the sectarian movements. Thus when I came to America twenty years ago [in 1933], the theology of the Reformation was almost unknown in Union Theological Seminary [New York] because of the different traditions, and the reduction of the Protestant tradition nearer to the non-Reformation traditions. Luther's conflict with the Evangelical Radicals is especially important for American Protestants because the prevailing type of Christianity in America was not produced by the Reformation directly, but by the indirect effect of the Reformation through the movement of Evangelical Radicalism.[281]

The last two decades have more than justified the observations of Bouyer and Tillich. The historical drift toward Rome has become like that place in the Niagara River where the boats reach the point of no return as the water rushes on toward the falls. The drift has accelerated into a race, and Evangelicals and Charismatics are re-entering Rome at an ever-increasing rate.

The Neo-Pentecostal, or Charismatic, Movement

From 1900 to 1960, the Pentecostal movement continued to grow outside the mainstream of Protestantism. Yet by 1960 it had attained a world-wide membership of about eight million. At that time, men like Henry Van Dusen began to call the movement the "Third Force" in Christendom.

Then about 1960 a remarkable change took place. Pentecostalism began to jump the denominational boundary lines and to penetrate the mainline Protestant churches. As John Sherrill says in his book, *They Speak With Other Tongues*, "the walls came tumbling down." Soon there were thousands, and then millions of Episcopalian, Methodist, Lutheran, Baptist, Presbyterian, Congregationalist and other Protestant Pentecostals. This interdenominational phase of the movement became known as the neo-Pentecostal, or Charismatic, movement. It was no longer a separate denomination but an experience that transcended all denominational boundary lines. Those having the experience in different denominations saw themselves as having more in common with each other than with non-Charismatics of the same church. Many confidently predicted that this was the beginning of the greatest revival the world had ever known.

Toward the end of the 1960's, the neo-Pentecostal movement made two further astounding strides. It entered the new youth culture and became known as the "Jesus Movement." It was estimated that ninety percent of the "Jesus people," as they were called, had some form of Pentecostal experience. Many from the drug culture became "high" on Jesus instead of drugs. Then to crown its success, the Charismatic movement entered the Roman Catholic church in 1967. After a modest beginning in its great centers of learning in America, Duquesne and Notre Dame Universities, it is now spreading rapidly in the Roman Catholic church, attracting the support of nuns, priests, bishops, cardinals, and the Popes themselves. Since Roman Catholics are now receiving the identical Pentecostal experience as Protestants, the old-line Pentecostals have been re-evaluating their attitude toward Roman Catholicism. Traditionally anti-papal, the classical Pentecostal churches are changing their position since "pentecost" has come to Rome.

Although Pentecostalism was introduced to the Roman Catholic church initially by Protestant Pentecostals, it is meeting even less resistance in Catholic circles than in Protestant circles. In fact, as many Catholic authors are pointing out, Pentecostalism is more at home in the ancient church. It is more at home there because the overwhelming Pentecostal emphasis on subjective experience is in essential harmony with the teaching and tradition of the Roman church. Says Benedictine monk Edward O'Connor of Notre Dame:

> Although they derive from Protestant background, the Pentecostal churches are not typically Protestant in their beliefs, attitudes or practices. ... [I]t cannot be assumed that the Pentecostal movement represents an incursion of Protestant influence [into the Roman Catholic church].
> ... Catholics who have accepted Pentecostal spirituality have found it to be fully in harmony with their traditional faith and life. They experience it, not as a borrowing from an alien religion, but as a connatural development of their own.
> ... [T]he experience of the Pentecostal movement tends to confirm the validity and relevance of our authentic spiritual traditions.
> Moreover, the doctrine that is developing in the Pentecostal churches today seems to be going through stages very similar to those which occurred in the early Middle Ages when the classical doctrine was taking shape.[282]

Moreover, neo-Pentecostalism certainly does nothing to unsettle the faith of Roman Catholics in their church and traditions. Says O'Connor:

> Similarly, the traditional devotions of the Church have taken on more meaning. Some people have been brought back to a frequent use of the sacrament of Penance through the experience of the baptism of the Spirit. Others have discovered a place for devotion to Mary in their lives, whereas previously they had been indifferent or even antipathetic toward her. One of the most striking effects of the Holy Spirit's action has been to stir up devotion to the Real Presence in the Eucharist.[283]

The Charismatic Movement and Rome

The 1970s brought us to a great ecumenical phase of revivalism and the Charismatic movement. On February 1, 1972, *Christianity Today* editorialized:

> The force that appears to be making the greatest contribution to the current Christian revival around the globe is Pentecostalism. This movement, which began several decades ago, and which in its early years was very sectarian in character, is now becoming ecumenical in the deepest sense. A neo-Pentecostalism has lately appeared that includes many thousands of Roman Catholics.... A new era of the Spirit has begun. The charismatic experience moves Christians far beyond glossolalia.... There is light on the horizon. An evangelical renaissance is becoming visible along the Christian highway from the frontiers of the sects to the high places of the Roman Catholic communion. This appears to be one of the most strategic moments in the Church's history.

The May 1972 issue of *New Covenant*, a Catholic Charismatic publication, features Catholics and Protestants uniting in a great Charismatic fellowship. It proclaims that the Charismatic movement holds the hope of healing the wound of the sixteenth century. Henry Van Dusen of Union Theological Seminary is featured as saying:

> The presence of the charismatic (Pentecostal) movement among us is said to make a new era in the development of Christianity. The new Pentecostalism will appear to future historians as a "true reformation" (compared to that of the sixteenth century) from which will spring a third force in the Christian world (Protestant-Catholic-Pentecostal.)[284]

This union is not based on objective truth but on subjective experience. American Christianity is drowning in a sea of religious subjectivism. Charismatic literature (and with it we include all this subjective revivalism) is infesting the land like the frogs of Egypt.[285] Never has such a mass of literature been so devoid of the Gospel of Christ. There is scarcely one objective thought in it. It is all "'in and in and in," a return to sentimental, effeminate, medieval, mysticism. No wonder one of the points of dialogue between Pentecostal leaders and the Roman Catholic church is the remarkable similarity between Pentecostalism and Catholic mysticism. The startling fact of the crumbling of Protestant resistance to the Charismatic movement illustrates the decadence of the Protestant churches. Even the word Protestant is becoming a dirty word. And to be critical of Catholicism is now an obscenity in Evangelical circles.

A Fulfillment of Prophecy

Multitudes are exulting that the church is being stirred by the fires of revivalism. This is not a passing fad but a remarkable fulfillment of Biblical prophecy.

Protestants once generally accepted the fact that the leopard-like beast of Revelation 13 was a symbol of the Papacy, which had dominated European civilization for about one thousand years. Armed with the objective truth of justification by faith, the Reformation gave the "man of sin" a "deadly wound." In breaking the stranglehold of Papal thought, it set the nations free from Papal domination.[286] But the prophecy of Revelation clearly foretells a restoration of the power of the ancient church to dominate the minds and enslave the consciences of men. The apostle John declares:

> He performs great signs, so that he even makes fire come down from heaven on the earth in the sight of men. And he deceives those who dwell on the earth by those signs which he was granted to do in the sight of the beast, telling those who dwell on the earth to make an image of the beast who was wounded by the sword and lived.[287]

"Fire from heaven in the sight of men" is an astoundingly accurate picture of the Charismatic movement. Fire is its favorite symbol—and it is the symbol God uses to describe that movement because it is a counterfeit outpouring of the Holy Spirit. It is not really fire from Heaven, but it appears to be fire from Heaven. It is "fire from heaven in the sight of men." But by its influence it will cause "those who dwell on the earth to make an image of the beast who was wounded by the sword and lived."

The last days of the world are to marked by great religious deceptions. Working in the guise of "fire from heaven" (the baptism of the Holy Spirit), "the spirits of demons" will perform "signs which go out to the kings of earth and of the whole world, to gather them to the battle of that great day of God Almighty."[288]

Already it is considered blasphemy to speak against the supernatural working within the Charismatic movement. A spirit of boastful certainty and arrogant intolerance has often been manifested by those who "have the spirit." The preoccupation with inward experience is leading multitudes back to the religious philosophy of the Dark Ages and the medieval church. The Vatican knows the score. It reads what is, and what is to be. Many Protestants seem to be as paralyzed as Melanchthon was when he did not know whether or not to speak out against the spiritualistic fanatics who came to Wartburg Castle. It was this issue that led the great Reformer to come out of hiding and to risk his life. Cried the spirit-filled leaders on being granted an interview with Luther, "The Spirit! The Spirit!" The Reformer was unimpressed. "I slap your spirit on the snout," he thundered. He understood that the great truth of justification by faith was diametrically opposed to these "German prophets," as he called them.

We have come now to the time when the issues of the sixteenth century have to be fought out again. This time the conflict will be more severe, and it will be final. Roll up the old denominational boundary lines. There is going to be a regrouping of the religious world. On the one side there will be a grand union of Roman Catholics, pseudo-Protestants, and Charismatics in what appears to be a movement for the conversion of the whole world. On the other side there will be a movement to restore the everlasting Gospel in its pristine purity and power. The Gospel will triumph. Though Antichrist may be victorious for a moment, his doom is sure. One little Word shall fell him.

Notes

1. *Who's Who in America, 1984-1985*, Volume 2. I have expanded some of the abbreviations to make the entry more intelligible.

2. Pat Robertson, *America's Dates With Destiny* (Nashville, Tennessee: Thomas Nelson Company, 1986), p. 18. Hereafter cited as *America's Dates*.

3. *America's Dates*, p. 19.

4. See the full account in Pat Robertson, with Jamie Buckingham, *Shout It From The Housetops* (South Plainfield, New Jersey: Bridge Publishing, 1972), pp. 20-25. Hereafter cited as *Shout*.

5. *Shout*, pp. 32-33.

6. T.R. Reid, "Robertson's Bid Powered by Faith, Self-Assurance," *The Washington Post*, September 11, 1987, p.1. The full account is found in Robertson's autobiography, *Shout It From The Housetops*, pp. 31-33.

7. *America's Dates*, p. 19.

8. *The New York Times*, December 10, 1986, p. B11.

9. J. Gresham Machen, *Christianity and Liberalism* (Grand Rapids, Michigan: Wm. B. Eerdmans Publishing Company, 1972 [1923]), p. 2.

10. John 17:17.

11. Matthew 4:4, 7, 10.

12. For further study on this point, see Gordon H. Clark, *God's Hammer: The Bible and Its Critics* (Jefferson, Maryland: The Trinity Foundation, 1987).

13. Hebrews 1:1, 2.

14. 2 Peter 1:15-21.

15. Romans 15:4.

16. Quoted in Loraine Boettner, *Roman Catholicism* (Philadelphia, Pennsylvania: Presbyterian and Reformed Publishing Company, 1974 [1962]), p. 97.

17. Pat Robertson, with William Proctor, *Beyond Reason: How Miracles Can Change Your Life* (New York: William Morrow and Company, 1985), p. 177. Hereafter cited as *Beyond Reason*.

18. Pat Robertson, *The Flame* (monthly newsletter of the Christian Broadcasting Network), Christmas 1980, n.p.

19. 2 Peter 1:16.

20. Hebrews 12:2.

21. John 17:4; 19:30.

22. John 17:12.

23. On this extremely important aspect of the Gospel, which virtually all modern churches deny, see Loraine Boettner, *The Reformed Doctrine of Predestination* (Phillipsburg, New Jersey: Presbyterian and Reformed Publishing Company, 1981 [1932]); and John Calvin, *Calvin's Calvinism* (Grand Rapids, Michigan: Reformed Free Publishing Association, 1987).

24. On this point see Gary D. Long, *Definite Atonement* (Nutley, New Jersey: Presbyterian and Reformed Publishing Company, 1977).

25. Matthew 1:21.

26. John 10:15.

27. John 15:13.

28. Ephesians 5:23-26; Acts 20:28.

29. Luke 24:27, 31-32, 45.

30. Many books have been published that refute the puerile criticisms of atheists that the Bible contradicts itself. Three of the better books are John W. Haley, *An Examination of the Alleged Discrepancies of the Bible* (Grand Rapids, Michigan: Baker Book House, 1977 [1874]); George W. DeHoff, *Alleged Bible Contradictions Explained* (Grand Rapids, Michigan: Baker Book House, 1970); and Gleason L. Archer, *Encyclopedia of Bible Difficulties* (Grand Rapids, Michigan: Zondervan Publishing House, 1982).

31. Micah 5:2.

32. Isaiah 7:14.

33. Isaiah 53:9, 12.

34. John 2:19.

35. Acts 20:27.

36. Matthew 4.

37. Genesis 3:6.

38. 2 Peter 1:16-19.

39. 2 Peter 1:3.

40. 2 Peter 1:19.

41. *The Westminster Confession of Faith*, Chapter 1, section 6.

42. Anthony A. Hoekema, *The Four Major Cults* (Grand Rapids, Michigan: Eerdmans Publishing Company, 1963), pp. 378-379.

43. Pat Robertson, with Bob Slosser, *The Secret Kingdom*, expanded edition (Nashville, Tennessee: Thomas Nelson Publishers, 1987 [1982]), pp. 232-233.

44. *The Secret Kingdom*, p. 234.

45. *Beyond Reason*, p. 40.

46. *The Secret Kingdom*, p. 235.

47. *Beyond Reason*, p. 94.

48. Pat Robertson, *The Secret Kingdom*, p. 243.

49. *Shout*, p. 82.
50. *Shout*, pp. 110-111.
51. *Shout*, p. 229.
52. *The Flame* (monthly newsletter of CBN), April 1978, p. 7.
53. *Shout*, pp. 198-199.
54. Pat Robertson, *Answers to 200 of Life's Most Probing Questions* (Nashville, Tennessee: Thomas Nelson Company, 1984), pp. 217-218. Hereafter cited as *Answers*.
55. *Answers*, p. 218.
56. *The Secret Kingdom*, pp. 67-68.
57. *Shout*, pp. 131-132.
58. *Shout*, p. 239.
59. *Shout*, p. 56.
60. *Shout*, pp. 69-70.
61. *Shout*, p. 82.
62. *Answers*, p. 218.
63. Deuteronomy 13:1-5.
64. For those readers who have an interest in the philosophy of science, the Bible taught the correct view of scientific method more than 3000 years before twentieth century philosophers came to similar conclusions. No number of successful experiments can prove a scientific hypothesis, but one unsuccessful experiment can destroy it.
65. Quoted in Victor Budgen, *The Charismatics and the Word of God: A Biblical and Historical Perspective on the Charismatic Movement* (Welwyn, Hertfordshire, England: Evangelical Press, 1985), p. 11.
66. Page 1.
67. *Pat Robertson's Perspective*, March 1978, p. 4.
68. *Pat Robertson's Perspective*, November 1979, p. 2.
69. *Pat Robertson's Perspective*, Special Issue, 1982, pp. 5-6.
70. *Pat Robertson's Perspective*, December 1977, p. 1.
71. *The Flame*, January 1980, p. 2.
72. *The Flame*, December 1979, p. 2.
73. *Pat Robertson's Perspective*, Special Issue, 1982, p. 4.
74. *Pat Robertson's Perspective*, Fall 1980, p. 5.
75. *Pat Robertson's Perspective*, Summer 1982, p. 1.
76. *700 Club* broadcast.
77. *The Wall Street Journal*, October 17, 1985.
78. *The Flame*, September 1980, n.p.
79. *The Flame*, March 1979, p. 3.
80. Revelation 22:18-19.
81. *Beyond Reason*, p. 177.

82. *Beyond Reason*, p. 12.
83. *Beyond Reason*, p. 53.
84. William Nolen, *Healing: A Doctor in Search of a Miracle* (New York: Random House, 1974), p. 60; as quoted in John F. MacArthur, Jr., *The Charismatics: A Doctrinal Perspective* (Grand Rapids, Michigan: Zondervan Publishing, 1978), p. 137.
85. Nolen, *Healing*, p. 107; as quoted in MacArthur, *The Charismatics*, p. 139.
86. Nolen, *Healing*, p. 104; as quoted in MacArthur, *The Charismatics*, p. 140.
87. *Beyond Reason*, pp. 170-171.
88. *The Secret Kingdom*, pp. 65-67.
89. *The Secret Kingdom*, p. 68.
90. *The Secret Kingdom*, pp. 68-69.
91. *The Secret Kingdom*, p. 221.
92. *Beyond Reason*, 1987, p. 20.
93. *The Secret Kingdom*, 1987, pp. 247-248.
94. *Beyond Reason*, p. 100.
95. *Beyond Reason*, pp. 103-104.
96. *Beyond Reason*, pp. 172-173.
97. See Exodus 8:18-19.
98. Deuteronomy 13:1-3,5.
99. Matthew 24:24.
100. Matthew 7:21-23.
101. 2 Thessalonians 2:9-10.
102. Revelation 13:11-14.
103. Revelation 16:13-14.
104. Revelation 19:20.
105. Galatians 1: 6-9.
106. 2 Corinthians 11:13-15.
107. John 10:41.
108. Acts 2:43.
109. Acts 5:12.
110. 2 Corinthians 12:12.
111. Acts 8:18-19.
112. 1 Timothy 5:23.
113. Benjamin Warfield, *Counterfeit Miracles* (London: The Banner of Truth Trust, 1972 [1918]), p. 83.
114. *Counterfeit Miracles*, pp. 93-94.
115. *Answers*, pp. 249-250.
116. *Counterfeit Miracles*, p. 124.

117. *The Flame*, February 1978, p. 2.
118. *The Secret Kingdom*, p. 68.
119. *The Secret Kingdom*, p. 73.
120. *The Secret Kingdom*, p. 79.
121. Acts 9:16.
122. 2 Corinthians 12:7-10.
123. 2 Corinthians 11:23-27.
124. John 15:20.
125. *The Secret Kingdom*, p. 69.
126. Dave Hunt, *Beyond Seduction: A Return to Biblical Christianity* (Eugene, Oregon: Harvest House Publishers, 1987), pp. 51-53.
127. *Beyond Reason*, p. 20.
128. *The Secret Kingdom*, pp. 66-67.
129. *The Secret Kingdom*, pp. 68-69.
130. *Beyond Reason*, p. 100.
131. *The Secret Kingdom*, p. 15.
132. *Answers*, p. 271.
133. *The Secret Kingdom*, p. 74.
134. *The Secret Kingdom*, p. 74.
135. 1 Corinthians 13:8-12.
136. *Shout*, p. 135.
137. 1 Corinthians 15:24.
138. James 1:4; 1 John 4:18; James 1:25; James 1:17; Hebrews 9:11; Romans 12:2; Hebrews 5:14; Ephesians 4:13; 1 Corinthians 14:20; 1 Corinthians 2:6; Philippians 3:15; Colossians 1:28; Matthew 5:48; Matthew 19:21; James 3:2; Colossians 4:12.
139. Douglas Judisch, *An Evaluation of Claims to the Charismatic Gifts* (Grand Rapids, Michigan: Baker Biblical Monograph, 1978), p. 83; as quoted in Victor Budgen, *The Charismatics and the Word of God*, p. 77.
140. Compare Numbers 7:89.
141. This discussion is deeply indebted to Victor Budgen. For a fuller discussion, the reader may want to consult his book, *The Charismatics and the Word of God*.
142. Richard Quebedeaux, *The New Charismatics II* (San Francisco: Harper and Row, 1983), p. 234.
143. Chrysostom, "Homilies on I Corinthians," *The Nicene and Post-Nicene Fathers*, Vol. XII.
144. "Speaking in Tongues," Vol. XI.
145. See Leonard Arrington and Davis Bitton, *The Mormon Experience* (New York: Vintage Books, 1980 [1979]), p. 87.
146. Quoted in Robert G. Gromacki, *The Modern Tongues Movement* (Philadelphia: Presbyterian and Reformed Publishing Company, 1972 [1967]), pp. 22-23.

147. Paul G. Hiebert, "Discerning the Work of God," *Charismatic Experiences in History*, Cecil M. Robeck, Jr., editor (Peabody, Massachusetts: Hendrickson Publishers, 1985), pp. 150-151.
148. Acts 2:4-6, 11.
149. *Shout*, p. 17.
150. *Shout*, p. 33.
151. *Shout*, p. 40.
152. *Shout*, pp. 97-98.
153. *Shout*, pp. 126-127.
154. *Shout*, p. 196.
155. *Answers*, pp. 216-217.
156. *Answers*, pp. 109-110.
157. *Answers*, p. 102.
158. *Answers*, p. 55.
159. Romans 5:12-21.
160. 1 Corinthians 15:45.
161. Luke 3:23-38.
162. 1 Corinthians 15:17.
163. Psalm 119:105.
164. Psalm 119:133.
165. Matthew 12:39.
166. The best book on divine guidance is *Decision Making and the Will of God*, Garry Friesen with J. Robin Maxson (Portland, Oregon: Multnomah Press, 1980). It is available from The Trinity Foundation.
167. Chapter 2, section 1.
168. *The Secret Kingdom*, p. 83.
169. Isaiah 40:15-17, 22-23.
170. Isaiah 45:5-7.
171. *Answers*, p. 26.
172. *Answers*, p. 48.
173. *Answers*, p. 26.
174. *Answers*, p. 27.
175. *Answers*, p. 88.
176. *Answers*, p. 95.
177. Galatians 3:24; see also Romans 7.
178. The reader is urged to consult Martin Luther's *The Bondage of the Will*.
179. Proverbs 21:1.
180. Romans 3:10-12.
181. Romans 3:23.

182. Psalm 51:5.
183. Genesis 1:31.
184. *Answers*, p. 57.
185. *Answers*, pp. 57-58.
186. Romans 3:19.
187. Romans 5:12.
188. *Answers*, p. 20.
189. Ephesians 1:11.
190. Proverbs 16:4.
191. Daniel 4:34-35.
192. *Answers*, p. 22.
193. *Answers*, p. 22.
194. *Answers*, p. 23.
195. Job 1:9-12.
196. 2 Corinthians 12:7-10.
197. Jonah 4:7-11.
198. James 1:2-4.
199. John 9:1-3.
200. Hebrews 12:5-9.
201. *Answers*, pp. 58-59.
202. *Answers*, p. 64.
203. Romans 10:17.
204. Hebrews 11:6.
205. Romans 9:13.
206. Proverbs 16:4.
207. Romans 9:21-24.
208. *Answers*, p. 82.
209. *Answers*, pp. 98-99.
210. Fundraising letter sent by Robertson to his supporters, quoted in Robert Walters, "Robertson's Holy Crusade," *The Frederick Post*, Frederick, Maryland, July 28, 1986.
211. *Christianity Today*, January 17, 1986, p. 34.
212. Letter dated "Thursday morning," presumably September 18, 1986, announcing Pat Robertson's decision to seek the Republican nomination for the presidency if "3 million registered voters sign petitions committing to pray, to work, and to give. . . ." The letter appeared on "Americans For Robertson" stationery, P.O. Box 37002, Washington, D.C. 20013.
213. Robert Walters, "Robertson's Holy Crusade," *The Frederick Post*, Frederick, Maryland, July 28, 1986.
214. Cecil M. Robeck, Jr., "Prophetic Authority in the Charismatic Setting: The Need to

Test," *Theological Renewal*, July 1983, p. 4; as quoted in Paul G. Hiebert, "Discerning the Work of God," *Charismatic Experiences in History*, p. 152.

215. Paul G. Hiebert, "Discerning the Work of God," *Charismatic Experiences in History*, p. 152.

216. *The Charismatics: A Doctrinal Perspective*, p. 15.

217. Acts 17:11.

218. Interview with Robertson in *U.S. News and World Report*, 1985, p. 71.

219. *The Secret Kingdom*, p. 155.

220. *The Secret Kingdom*, p. 148.

221. Page 4.

222. *Pat Robertson's Perspective*, Fall 1980, pp. 3-4.

223. *The Wall Street Journal*, December 26, 1986, p. 26.

224. *700 Club*, July 15, 1982.

225. *Pat Robertson's Perspective*, January/February 1981, p. 3.

226. The leading lights of both movements are Gary North and Ronald Sider, respectively.

227. *Westminster Confession of Faith*, chapter 19.

228. *The Secret Kingdom*, p. 152.

229. *Pat Robertson's Perspective*, January/February 1981, p. 3.

230. *Answers*, pp. 194-196.

231. *Answers*, p. 263.

232. *Answers*, p. 21.

233. *The Secret Kingdom*, p. 22.

234. *The Secret Kingdom*, p. 13.

235. *The Secret Kingdom*, p. 94.

236. *Answers*, p. 189.

237. Pat Robertson, "Toward a Community of Democratic Nations," *The Fletcher Forum*, Summer 1987, pp. 260-261.

238. See John W. Robbins, *War and Peace: A Christian Foreign Policy* (Jefferson, Maryland: The Trinity Foundation, 1988), forthcoming.

239. Pat Robertson, "Dictatorships and Single Standards," *Policy Review*, Winter 1987, p. 2.

240. "Dictatorships and Single Standards," p. 2.

241. "Dictatorships and Single Standards," pp. 5, 7.

242. *Answers*, p. 192.

243. *Pat Robertson's Perspective*, April 1979, pp. 3-4.

244. Exodus 20:15.

245. 1 Kings 21.

246. Mark 6:14-29.

247. Luke 19.

248. *The Secret Kingdom*, pp. 121-122.

249. May 1, 1986, *700 Club* appearance.

250. Matthew 20:25-28; compare Luke 22:25-27.

251. See John W. Robbins, *The Pursuit of Power: Dominion Theology and the Reconstruction Movement* (Jefferson, Maryland: The Trinity Foundation, 1988), forthcoming.

252. *Answers*, p. 192.

253. *Pat Robertson's Perspective*, January/February 1979, p.4.

254. Deuteronomy 6:6-7.

255. Ephesians 6:4.

256. Soren Kierkegaard, *Journals*.

257. Friedrich Schleiermacher, *On Religion: Speeches to its Cultured Despisers* (New York: Harper and Row, 1958), p. 105.

258. John L. Sherrill, *They Speak With Other Tongues* (New York: Pyramid Books, 1967 [1964]), p. 10.

259. *They Speak With Other Tongues*, p. 11.

260. John Wimber, with Kevin Springer, *Power Evangelism* (San Francisco: Harper and Row, 1986), p. 74.

261. Matthew 22:23-28.

262. Matthew 22:29-32.

263. John 3:10.

264. Matthew 22:33.

265. *Power Evangelism*, p. 74.

266. *The Westminster Assembly and Its Work* (Cherry Hill, New Jersey: Mack Publishing Company, 1972), pp. 226-227.

267. Matthew 12:14.

268. Matthew 12:25-28.

269. Frank Bartleman, quoted in Frederick Dale Bruner, *A Theology of the Holy Spirit* (Grand Rapids, Michigan: Wm. B. Eerdmans Publishing, 1983 [1970]) p. 120.

270. Michael Harper, *As at the Beginning* (London: Hodder, 1967), p. 110; as quoted in *The Charismatics and the Word of God*, p. 63.

271. Raymond Frame, "Something Unusual," *HIS*, December 1963, p. 27; as quoted in Robert G. Gromacki, *The Modern Tongues Movement*, p. 151.

272. *Answers*, p. 207.

273. *Shout*, pp. 14-15.

274. This essay is an extensively revised and adapted version of an anonymous pamphlet published in 1972 by the Australian Forum. The Forum no longer publishes the magazine in which the original essay appeared, *Present Truth*, and it seems to have repudiated the theology of the original essay as well. The original title was "Protestantism, the Pentecostal Movement, and the Drift Back to Rome."

275. *What Luther Says* (St. Louis, Missouri: Concordia Publishing House, 1959), Vol. 2, pp. 702-704.

276. John Wesley, *A Plain Account of Christian Perfection* (Chicago: Christian Witness, n.d.), p. 7.

277. Vinson Synan, *The Holiness-Pentecostal Movement in the United States* (Grand Rapids, Michigan: Wm. B. Eerdmans Publishing Company, 1971), p. 25.

278. *A Theology of the Holy Spirit*, p. 44.

279. Kilian McDonnell, "The Classical Pentecostal Movement," *New Covenant*, May 1972, p. 1.

280. Louis Bouyer, *The Spirit and Forms of Protestantism* (Cleveland, Ohio: World Publishing Company, 1964), pp. 186, 188, 189, 197.

281. Paul Tillich, *A History of Christian Thought* (London: S.C.M. Press, 1968), pp. 225-226, 238.

282. Edward O'Connor, *The Pentecostal Movement in the Catholic Church* (Notre Dame, Indiana: Ave Maria Press, 1971), pp. 23, 32, 28, 183, 191, 193, 194.

283. Edward O'Connor, *Pentecost in the Catholic Church* (Pecos, New Mexico: Dove Publications, 1970), pp. 14, 15.

284. *New Covenant*, May 1972, p. 19.

285. Revelation 16:13, 14.

286. Revelation 13:3.

287. Revelation 13:13-14.

288. Revelation 16:14. See also 2 Thessalonians 2:8-12.

Sources

Archer, Gleason L. *Encyclopedia of Bible Difficulties*. Grand Rapids, Michigan: Zondervan Publishing House, 1982.

Arrington, Leonard J. and Davis Bitton. *The Mormon Experience: A History of the Latter-day Saints*. New York: Vintage Books, 1980 [1979].

Baxter, Ronald E. *The Charismatic Gift of Tongues*. Grand Rapids, Michigan: Kregel Publications, 1981.

Boettner, Loraine. *The Reformed Doctrine of Predestination*. Phillipsburg, New Jersey: Presbyterian and Reformed Publishing Company, 1981 [1932].

Boettner, Loraine, *Roman Catholicism*. Philadelphia, Pennsylvania: Presbyterian and Reformed Publishing Company, 1962.

Bruner, Frederick Dale. *A Theology of the Holy Spirit: The Pentecostal Experience and the New Testament Witness*. Grand Rapids, Michigan: Wm. B. Eerdmans, 1983 [1970].

Budgen, Victor, *The Charismatics and the Word of God: A Biblical and Historical Perspective on the Charismatic Movement*. Welwyn, Hertfordshire, England: Evangelical Press, 1985.

Calvin, John. *Calvin's Calvinism*. Grand Rapids, Michigan: Reformed Free Publishing Association, 1987.

Clark, Gordon H. *The Biblical Doctrine of Man*. Jefferson, Maryland: The Trinity Foundation, 1984.

Clark, Gordon H. *A Christian Philosophy of Education*. Jefferson, Maryland: The Trinity Foundation, 1988.

Clark, Gordon H. *A Christian View of Men and Things*. Grand Rapids, Michigan: Baker Book House, 1982 [1952].

Clark, Gordon H. *Faith and Saving Faith*. Jefferson, Maryland: The Trinity Foundation, 1983.

Clark, Gordon H. *God's Hammer: The Bible and Its Critics*. Jefferson, Maryland: The Trinity Foundation, 1987 [1982].

Clark, Gordon H. *Predestination*. Phillipsburg, New Jersey: Presbyterian and Reformed Publishing Company, 1987.

Clark, Gordon H. *Religion, Reason and Revelation*. Jefferson, Maryland: The Trinity Foundation, 1986.

Clark, Gordon H. *What Do Presbyterians Believe?* Phillipsburg, New Jersey: Presbyterian and Reformed Publishing Company, 1986 [1965].

DeHoff, George W. *Alleged Bible Contradictions Explained*. Grand Rapids, Michigan: Baker Book House, 1970.

Friesen, Garry and J. Robin Maxson. *Decision-Making and the Will of God*. Portland, Oregon: Multnomah Press, 1980.

Gromacki, Robert G. *The Modern Tongues Movement*. Philadelphia, Pennsylvania: Presbyterian and Reformed Publishing Company, 1972 [1967].

Haley, John W. *An Examination of the Alleged Discrepancies of the Bible*. Grand Rapids, Michigan: Baker Book House, 1977 [1874].

Hoekema, Anthony A. *The Four Major Cults*. Grand Rapids, Michigan: Wm. B. Eerdmans Publishing Company, 1974 [1963].

Hunt, Dave. *Beyond Seduction: A Return to Biblical Christianity*. Eugene, Oregon: Harvest House Publishers, 1987.

Hunt, Dave, and T.A. McMahon. *The Seduction of Christianity: Spiritual Discernment in the Last Days*. Eugene, Oregon: Harvest House Publishers, 1985.

Kinchlow, Ben, with Bob Slosser. *Plain Bread*. Waco, Texas: Word Books, 1985.

Long, Gary D. *Definite Atonement*. Nutley, New Jersey: Presbyterian and Reformed Publishing Company, 1977.

MacArthur, John F. Jr. *The Charismatics: A Doctrinal Perspective*. Grand Rapids, Michigan: Zondervan Publishing House, 1978.

Machen, J. Gresham. *Christianity and Liberalism*. Grand Rapids, Michigan: Wm. B. Eerdmans Publishing Company, 1972 [1923].

Machen, J. Gresham. *Education, Christianity and the State*. Jefferson, Maryland: The Trinity Foundation, 1987.

Nolen, William. *Healing: A Doctor in Search of a Miracle*. New York; Random House, 1974.

Quebedeaux, Richard. *By What Authority: The Rise of Personality Cults in American Christianity*. San Francisco: Harper and Row, 1982.

Quededeaux, Richard. *The New Charismatics: The Origins, Development, and Significance of Neo-Pentecostalism*. New York: Doubleday and Company, 1976.

Quebedeaux, Richard. *The New Charismatics II*. San Francisco: Harper and Row, 1983.

Robbins, John W. *The Pursuit of Power: Dominion Theology and The Reconstruction Movement*. Jefferson, Maryland: The Trinity Foundation, 1988.

Robbins, John W. *War and Peace: A Christian Foreign Policy*. Jefferson, Maryland: The Trinity Foundation, 1988.

Robeck, Cecil M., Jr. *Charismatic Experiences in History*. Peabody, Massachusetts: Hendrickson Publishers, 1985.

Robertson, Pat. *America's Dates With Destiny*. Nashville, Tennessee: Thomas Nelson Publishers, 1986.

Robertson, Pat. *Answers to 200 of Life's Most Probing Questions*. Nashville, Tennessee: Thomas Nelson Company, 1984.

Robertson, Pat, with William Proctor, *Beyond Reason: How Miracles Can Change Your Life*. New York: William Morrow and Company, 1985.

Robertson, Pat. *My Prayer for You*. Old Tappan, New Jersey: Fleming H. Revell Company, 1977.

Robertson, Pat, with Bob Slosser. *The Secret Kingdom* (expanded edition). Nashville, Tennessee: Thomas Nelson Publishers, 1987 [1982].

Schleiermacher, Friedrich. *On Religion: Speeches to Its Cultured Despisers*. New York: Harper and Row, 1958.

Sherrill, John L. *They Speak With Other Tongues*. New York: Pyramid Books, 1967 [1964].

Straub, Gerard Thomas. *Salvation For Sale: An Insider's View of Pat Robertson's Ministry*. Buffalo, New York: Prometheus Books, 1986.

Warfield, Benjamin B. *Counterfeit Miracles*. London: The Banner of Truth Trust, 1972 [1918].

Warfield, Benjamin B. *The Westminster Assembly and Its Work*. Cherry Hill, New Jersey: Mack Publishing Company, 1972.

Wimber, John, with Kevin Springer. *Power Evangelism*. San Francisco: Harper and Row, 1986.

Scripture Index

Acts, *65*
  2, *61*
  2:4-6,11, *127n.148*
  2:22, *48*
  2:43, *48, 125n.108*
  5:12, *48, 125n.109*
  8:18-19, *125n.111*
  9:16, *51, 126n.121*
  17:11, *78, 129n.217*
  20:27, *21, 123n.35*
  20:28, *19, 123n.28*

1 Chronicles
  21, *91*

Colossians
  1:28, *126n.138*
  4:12, *126n.138*

1 Corinthians, *55*
  2:6, *126n.138*
  7:32, *62, 64*
  11:26, *55*
  13, *55, 56, 57*
  13:1, *61*
  13:8, *65*
  13:8-12, *126n.135*
  13:12, *56*
  14:2, *61*
  14:4, *61*
  14:5, *61*
  14:6, *61*
  14:9, *61*
  14:13, *61*
  14:14, *61*
  14:18, *61*
  14:19, *61*
  14:20, *126n.138*
  14:21, *61*
  14:22, *61*
  14:23, *61*
  14:26, *61*
  14:27, *61*
  14:39, *61*
  15, *18, 20, 21, 101*
  15:17, *127n.160*
  15:24, *55, 126n.137*
  15:26, *55*
  15:45, *127n.160*

2 Corinthians
  11:13-15, *30, 47, 125n.106*
  11:23-27, *51, 126n.123*
  12:7-10, *51, 72, 126n.122, 128n.196*
  12:12, *48, 125n.110*

Daniel
  4:34-35, *72, 128n.191*

Deuteronomy
  6:6-7, 95, 130n.254
  13, 32, 33, 46
  13:1-3, 5, 45, 125n.98
  13:1-5, 124n.63
  18:20-22, 31, 32
  20:5-8, 89-90
  29:29, 66
  34:10, 57

Ephesians
  1:11, 71, 128n.189
  4:13, 126n.138
  5:23-26, 19, 123n.28
  6:4, 95, 130n.225

Exodus
  4:1-5, 47-48
  8:18-19, 125n.97
  20:15, 88, 89, 129n.244
  21:16, 88
  33:9-11, 57

Galatians, 74
  1:6-9, 46, 125n.105
  3:24, 70, 127n.177

Genesis, 27, 65
  1:28, 93
  1:31, 127n.183
  3:6, 123n.37

Hebrews
  1:1-2, 10, 122n.13
  5:14, 126n.138
  9:11, 126n.138
  11:6, 74, 128n.204
  12:2, 19, 123n.20
  12:5-9, 72, 128n.200

Isaiah
  7:14, 20, 123n.32
  8:19-20, 46n.
  18:1, 96
  40:15-17, 68-69
  40:22-23, 69
  40:15-17, 22-23, 127n.169
  45:5-7, 69, 127n.170
  53:9, 12, 20, 123n.33

James
  1:2-4, 128n.198
  1:4, 126n.138
  1:17, 126n.138
  1:25, 126n.138
  3:2, 126n.138

Jeremiah
  14:14, 24
  16:2, 62, 64
  23:16, 24

Job
  1:9-12, 72, 128n.195

John
  2:19, 20, 123n.34
  3, 8
  3:10, 99, 130n.263
  4:35, 62
  4:53, 64
  8:47, 101
  9:1-3, 72, 128n.199
  9:41, 102
  10:15, 19, 123n.26
  10:41, 47, 125n.107
  15:13, 19, 123n.27
  15:20, 52, 126n.124
  17:4, 19, 123n.21
  17:12, 123n.22
  17:17, 10, 122n.10

18:36, *102*
19:30, *19, 123n.21*

1 John
4:18, *126n.138*

Jonah
4:7-11, *72, 128n.197*

1 Kings
1:21, *89*
6:37, *63, 64*
21, *129n.245*

Lamentations
3:38, *69*

Leviticus
25:8-55, *81*
25:29-30, *83*

Luke
3:23-38, *127n.161*
4:18, *33n.-34n.*
10, *15, 103*
19, *89, 129n.247*
22:25-27, *130n.250*
24:27, *123n.29*
24:31-32, *123n.29*
24:45, *123n.29*

Mark
6:14-29, *89, 129n.246*
8:36, *76*

Matthew
1:21, *19, 123n.25*
4, *123n.36*
4:4, 7, 10, *10, 122n.11*
5:48, *126n.138*
7:21-23, *45, 125n.100*

12:11-12, *102*
12:14, *130n.267*
12:25-26, *102*
12:25-28, *103, 130n.268*
12:69, *127n.165*
19:21, *126n.138*
20:25-28, *93, 130n.250*
22:23-28, *98, 130n.261*
22:29-32, *98, 130n.262*
22:33, *130n.264*
24:4-5, *18n.*
24:24, *45, 125n.99*

Micah
5:2, *20, 123n.31*

Numbers
7:89, *126n.140*
12:6-8, *56*

2 Peter
1:3, *6, 22, 123n.39*
1:15-21, *11, 122n.14*
1:16, *122n.19*
1:16-19, *22, 123n.38*
1:19, *123n.4*
1:20-21, *10*
3:16, *59*

Philippians
3:15, *126n.138*

Proverbs
16:4, *71, 74, 128n.190, 128n.206*
21:1, *70, 127n.179*
30:5-6, *24*

Psalms
51:5, *127n.182*
119:105, *127n.163*

119:133, *127n.164*

Revelation
13, *120*
13:3, *131n.286*
13:11-14, *45-46, 125n.102*
13:13-14, *131n.287*
16:13-14, *125n.103, 131n.285*
16:14, *131n.288*
19:20, *46, 125n.104*
22:18-19, *38, 124n.80*

Romans
3:10-12, *70, 127n.180*
3:19, *71, 128n.186*
3:23, *70, 127n.181*
5:12, *71, 128n.187*
5:12, 18, *18n.-19n.*
5:12-21, *66, 127n.159*
7, *99, 114, 127n.177*
8, *114*

9:13, *74, 128n.205*
9:21-24, *74, 128n.207*
10:17, *74, 128n.203*
12:2, *126n.138*
12:10, *19n.*
13:1-4, *94-95*
15:4, *12, 122n.15*

1 Samuel
8, *89, 91*
16:1, *64*

2 Thessalonians
2:8-12, *131n.288*
2:9-10, *45, 125n.101*

1 Timothy
5:23, *125n.112*

2 Timothy
3:14-17, *10*
3:16-17, *24*

Index

Abortion, 67
Abraham, 20, 48, 66, 98, 99, 100
Ad hominem argument, 102
Adam, 65, 66, 69, 70, 82
Aeneid (Virgil), 59-60
Agur, 43
Ahab, 88-89
Alleged Bible Contradictions Explained (George W. DeHoff), 123n.30
America's Dates With Destiny (Pat Robertson), 5, 16, 122n.2, n.3, n.7
Americans For Robertson, 4, 128n.212
Amos, 12
Anabaptists, 110
Ananias, 51
Answers to 200 of Life's Most Probing Questions (Pat Robertson), 16, 124n.54, n.55, n.62, 126n.132, 127n.155, n.156, n.157, n.158, n.171, n.172, n.173, n.174, n.175, n.176, 128n.184, n.185, n.188, n.192, n.193, n.194, n.201, n.202, n.208, n.209, 129n.230, n.231, n.232, n.236, n.242, 130n.252, n.272

Antichrist, 121
Apollo, 60
Archer, Gleason L., *Works: Encyclopedia of Bible Difficulties,* 123n.30
Arminianism, 100, 111, 113
Arrington, Leonard, and Davis Bitton, *Works: The Mormon Experience,* 126n.145
As at the Beginning (Michael Harper), 130n.270
Assemblies of God, 28
Atonement, 21, 112
Augustine, 70
Australian Forum, 130n.274

Babel, Tower of, 13
Bakker, Jim, xii, 28-29, 76
Bakker, Tammy, xii, 28
Banking system, 81
Bartleman, Frank, 130n.269
Beasts, 45-46, 120-121
Beelzebub, 103
Behaviorism, 97
Benjamin, 91
Berlin Wall, 33
Beyond Reason: How Miracles Can Change Your Life (Pat Robertson), 16, 122n.17,

123n.47, 124n.81, n.82, n.83, n.87, n.92, n.94, n.95, n.96, 126n.127, n.130
Beyond Seduction: A Return to Biblical Christianity (Dave Hunt), 126n.126
Bible, 6, 7, 8, 9, 11, 12, 14, 15, 16, 17, 18, 19, 20, 22, 23, 25, 26, 29, 31, 36, 37-38, 40, 49, 51, 52, 59-75, 78, 79, 83, 84, 85, 88-92, 97, 99, 104; completion of, 54-58; inspiration of, 10; logical arguments in, 98-103; Robertson's use of, 62-64
Bigotry, secular, xi
Bitton, Davis, and Leonard Arrington, Works: *The Mormon Experience*, 126n.145
Boardman, George Dana, 114
Boettner, Loraine, Works: *The Reformed Doctrine of Predestination*, 123n.23; *Roman Catholicism*, 122n.16
Bondage of the Will, The (Martin Luther), 127n.178
Bouyer, Louis, 116, 117; Works: *The Spirit and Forms of Protestantism*, 131n.280
Bredesen, Harald, 36-37
Bruner, Frederick Dale, 115; Works: *A Theology of the Holy Spirit*, 130n.269, 131n.278
Buckingham, Jamie, 1, 122n.4, n.5
Budgen, Victor, Works: *The Charismatics and the Word of God: A Biblical and Historical Perspective on the Charismatic Movement*, 124n65, 126n.139, n.141, 130n.270

Calvary, 21
Calvin, John, 91, 110, 113; Works: *Calvin's Calvinism*, 123n.23
Calvin's Calvinism (John Calvin), 123n.23
Calvinism, 112
Campaign for President, 76-77
Cancer cures, 40-41
Capital punishment, 88, 95
Capitalism, 83-85
Catholic, see Roman Catholic
CBN University, 4
Channeling, 31
Charismatic Experiences in History (Cecil M. Robeck, Jr.), 126n.147, 128n.214, 129n.215
Charismatic movement, xii, 23, 25, 59, 64, 77, 97-100, 103-105, 107-108, 109-121
Charismatics and the Word of God: A Biblical and Historical Perspective on the Charismatic Movement, The (Victor Budgen), 124n.65, 126n.139, n.141, 130n.270
Charismatics: A Doctrinal Perspective, The (John F. MacArthur), 125n.84, n.85, n.86
Christian Broadcasting Network, 3-4, 27, 30, 36, 37, 63, 64, 76, 77, 107, 122n.18, 124n.52
Christian Science, 7, 25
Christian's Secret of a Happy Life, The (Hannah Whitall Smith), 114
Christianity, definition of, 6-23; ridicule of, xii
Christianity and Liberalism (J. Gresham Machen), 122n.9

Christianity Today, 76, 119, 128n.211
Chrysostom, 60; *Works:* "Homilies on I Corinthians," 126n.143
Church, 12, 19
Church of Jesus Christ of Latter-Day Saints, *see* Mormons
Churchill, Gladys (Robertson), 2
Churchill, Winston, 2
Clark, Gordon H., *Works: God's Hammer: The Bible and Its Critics,* 122n.12; *What Do Presbyterians Believe?* 9
"Classical Pentecostal Movement, The," (Kilian McDonnell), 131n.279
Committee for Freedom, 4
Communism, 87
Conn, Charles, 115
Conscription, 88-92; *see also* Draft
Contracts, rewriting of, 80-83
Council for National Policy, 4
Council of Valencia, 12
Counterfeit Miracles (Benjamin Warfield), 125n.113, n.114, n.116
Covenant of Works, 82
Creation, 42, 52, 70; as allegory, 66
Cults, 23, 25-26
Curry Sound Corporation, 1

Dark Ages, 12, 23, 49-50, 109, 118, 121
David, King, 91, 113
Dead, Robertson's attempt to raise, 44
Death, 18n.-19n.
Debt, cancellation of, 80-83, 95

Decision Making and the Will of God (Garry Friesen with J. Robin Maxson), 127n.166
Decree, of God, denied by Robertson, 73
Definite Atonement (Gary D. Long), 123n.24
DeHoff, George W., *Works: Alleged Bible Contradictions Explained,* 123n.30
Demons, 15, 46, 59, 103, 121
Denying the antecedent, fallacy of, 33
Depression, 84; inaccurately predicted by Robertson, 34-35
Devil, *see* Satan
"Dictatorships and Single Standards," (Pat Robertson), 129n.239, n.240, n.241
"Discerning the Work of God," (Paul G. Hiebert), 125n.147, 128n.214, 129n.215
Dominion theology, xii, 14, 15, 22, 93-94
Draft, 88-92, 95; advocated by Robertson, 80; as solution for unemployment, 88; for juvenile delinquency, 88
Duquesne University, 118

East Germany, 36
Ecology, 85
Economic cycles, 34, 84
Education, 94=95
Eighth Commandment, 88-90
Election, doctrine of, 16, 19, 21
Elijah, 40, 47
Elisha, 40, 47
Encyclopedia of Bible Difficulties (Gleason L. Archer), 123n.30
Energy use, 85

Esau, 74
Ethiopia, 36
Evaluation of Claims to the Charismatic Gifts, An (Douglas Judisch), 126n.139
Evangelical, definition of, 13-14
Evangelicals, 23
Evangelicals for Social Action, 81
Evangelism, 15, 99-100
Eve, 22, 65
Evil, origin of, 69-70
Examination of the Alleged Discrepancies of the Bible, An (John W. Haley), 123n.30
Existentialism, 97
Experience, 19, 23, 29, 107, 109, 113; *see also* Experientialism, Religious Experience, *and* Subjectivism
Experientialism, 17
Ezekiel, 36

"Face to face," meaning of, 55-57
Faith, 7, 10, 14, 16, 19, 21, 25, 74; Robertson's laws of, 42, 52, 53
Fall of man, 71, 82
False apostles, 30, 47
False christs, 18, 45, 46
False gods, 18
False gospels, 14-15, 46
False ministers, 30, 47, 51
False prophets, 24, 32-34, 45, 46
False religions, 23
False teachers, 46
Fanaticism, 3, 77-79, 106, 107, 112, 121
Finney, Charles, 30-31, 113
Fire-Baptized Holiness Church, 115

Flame, The, 35, 37, 122n.18, 124n.52, n.71, n.72, 125n.117
Fletcher Forum, The, 86, 129n.237
Foreign aid, 92-93, 95
Foreign policy, 85-88, 108
Four Major Cults, The (Anthony A. Hoekema), 123n.42
Frame, Raymond, *Works:* "Something Unusual," 130n.271
Frederick Post, The, 128n.210, n.213
Free will, 69-74, 111
Freedom Council, 4
Freedoms Foundation, 1
Friesen, Garry, *Works: Decision Making and the Will of God,* 127n.166
Full Gospel Businessmen's Fellowship International, 43
Fuller Theological Seminary, 77
Fundamentalism, 21

Gabriel, 49
Gaither, Bill, 78
Gaither, Gloria, 78
Garden of Eden, 22, 42, 52
Gill, John, 55
God, xii, 3, 5, 6, 7, 8, 9, 10, 12, 14, 16, 18, 24, 25, 26, 27, 28, 30, 31, 32, 33, 35, 37, 39, 40, 41, 43, 45, 48, 54, 56, 57, 61, 63, 70, 74, 76, 82, 86, 91, 92, 94, 95, 98, 99, 107, 108, 110, 121; doctrine of, 68; foreknowledge of, 73; knowledge of, 6, 22; omnipotence of, 73; omniscience of, 73; sovereignty of, 68-75; *see also* Jesus Christ, God the Father, *and* Holy Spirit
God the Father, 11, 21, 22, 45, 50,

112; *see also* God, Jesus Christ, *and* Holy Spirit
God's Hammer: The Bible and Its Critics (Gordon H. Clark), 122n.12
Gordon Seminary, 63, 64
Gospel, 46, 52, 82, 101, 110, 112, 120, 121; counterfeit, 14-15; definition of, 13-19; distorted by Pietism, 111
Gossip (game), 11-12
Government, proper function of, 94-95; regulations, 93
Grace, 7, 74
Gromacki, Robert G., *Works: The Modern Tongues Movement*, 126n.146, 130n.271
Guidance, 26-38, 62-68, 76
Guideposts, 97

Haley, John W. *Works: An Examination of the Alleged Discrepancies of the Bible*, 123n.30
Hamlet, Prince of Denmark, 1
Harper, Michael, *Works: As at the Beginning*, 130n.270
Harrison, Benjamin, 2
Harrison, William Henry, 2
Healing, 15, 16, 40-42, 75; Mormon belief in, 60
Healing: A Doctor in Search of a Miracle (William Nolen), 40-41, 125n.84, n.85, n.86
Heaven, 11, 14, 15, 16, 47, 56, 121
Hell, 19, 46
Herod, 89
Hiebert, Paul G., 60; *Works:* "Discerning the Work of God," 126n.147, 128n.214, 129n.215

Hinduism, 60
HIS, 130n.271
History of Christian Thought, A (Paul Tillich), 131n.281
Hitler, Adolf, 86
Hoekema, Anthony A., *Works: The Four Major Cults*, 123n.42
Holiness movement, 112-114, 115
Holiness-Pentecostal Movement in the United States, The (Vinson Synan), 131n.277
Holy Spirit, 3, 10, 11, 14, 16, 17, 21, 23, 25, 26, 27, 29, 30, 31, 42, 43, 48, 49, 51, 52, 54, 60, 65, 74, 75, 77, 78, 103, 111-112, 115, 119, 121; baptism of, 14, 59; filling of, 14; *see also* God, God the Father, *and* Jesus Christ
"Homilies on I Corinthians," (Chrysostom), 126n.143
Humanism, 70
Hunt, Dave, 52; *Works: Beyond Seduction: A Return to Biblical Christianity*, 126n.126
Hunt, H.L., 30
Hurricane Betsy, stopped by Robertson, 43-44

I Believe in Miracles (Kathryn Kuhlman), 41
Index of Forbidden Books, Bible placed on by Roman Catholic church, 12
Inflation, 80, 81
Inspiration, definition of, 24
Insurance, 81
Interest, Robertson's opposition to, 83
Internal Revenue Service, 4
International police force, 86-88,

93, 95; advocated by Robertson, 80
Intervarsity Christian Fellowship, 3
Interventionism, in foreign policy, 87-88
Iran, 36
Irrationalism, 96-105
Irwin, Benjamin, 115
Isaac, 48, 98, 99, 100
Isaiah, 12, 46
Islam, 25
Israel, 35, 36, 81-82, 91

Jacob, 48, 74, 98, 99, 100
Jakeh, 43
Jeremiah, 12
Jesus Christ, xii, 2, 6-7, 10, 11, 14, 16, 19, 22, 23, 35, 40, 42, 44, 46, 47, 49, 50, 51, 52, 53, 56, 57, 63, 65, 74, 75, 97, 98, 99, 100, 103, 107, 112; birth predicted, 20; crucifixion of, 6; divinity of, 8; Gospel of, 18; death described, 19, 20; incarnation of God the Son, 6; resurrection of, 19; second coming of, 14, 36-37, 54, 55; temptation of, 21
Jesus Movement, 118
Joab, 91
Job, 72
John, 120
John the Baptist, 21, 37, 47, 52, 89
Johns Hopkins University, The, xii
Jonah, 72
Joshua, 40
Journals (Soren Kierkegaard), 130n.256
Jubilee, 34, 83-85, 91-92; advocated by Robertson, 80-83
Judas, 19, 74
Judgment, of God, 38
Judisch, Douglas, *Works: An Evaluation of Claims to the Charismatic Gifts*, 126n.139
Julius Caesar, 18
Jupiter effect, 35
Justification by faith alone, 7, 16, 109, 110, 111, 112-114, 116, 120-121

Kant, Immanuel, 96-97
Kemp, Jack, 77
Keswick Convention, 114
Keynes, John Maynard, 84
Keys to Victorious Living, 114
Kierkegaard, Soren, 96-97; *Works: Journals*, 130n.256
Kingdom of God (Heaven), 17, 102-103
Kingdom, laws of, 53
King Is Coming, The (Bill and Gloria Gaither), 78
Knowledge, of God, 6, 22
Kondratieff, N.D., 34, 84
Korean War, 87
Kuhlman, Kathryn, 40-41, 44-45; *Works: I Believe in Miracles*, 41

Laissez-faire, 83
Language, misuse of, 7
Law of Reciprocity, 92
Law, of God, 82-83
Law, purpose of, 69-70
Laxalt, Paul, 107
Lazarus, 20
Lear, Norman, 77
Lebanon, 36
Levi, 91
Liberalism, 97

Liberation theology, 81
Libya, 36
Lincoln, Abraham, xi, 6
Live Coals of Fire, 115
Logic, 25, 33, 96-105; in the Bible, 98-103
Long, Gary D., *Works: Definite Atonement,* 123n.24
Louis XIV, 35
Lourdes, 50
Love, 54, 92
Luke, 66, 78
Luther, Martin, 12, 110, 112, 113, 117, 121; *Works: The Bondage of the Will,* 127n.178
Lutheran church, 111
Lying, Robertson's definition of, 106

MacArthur, Douglas, 87
MacArthur, John, Jr., *Works: The Charismatics: A Doctrinal Perspective,* 78, 125n.84, n.85, n.86, 129n.216
Machen, J. Gresham, 7; *Works: Christianity and Liberalism,* 122n.9
"Making the world safe for democracy," 87
Man, 74
Mao Tse Tung, 86
Marshall, Catherine, 97
Marshall, Peter, 97
Marx, Karl, 84, 97
Mary, mother of Jesus, 6, 49, 50, 119
McCloskey, Paul, 4-5, 88
McDonnell, Kilian, 115; *Works:* "The Classical Pentecostal Movement," 131n.279
Means of production, redistribution of, advocated by Robertson, 80-83
Melancthon, Philip, 121
Methodism, 111-112, 113-114
Middle East, 35
Middle East Television, 4
Miracles, xii, 14, 15, 16, 17, 19, 22, 26, 32, 33, 39-58, 59, 65, 75, 80, 106, 120-121; disappearance of, 48-49; purpose of, 47; Satanic, 44-47
Modern Tongues Movement, The (Robert G. Gromacki), 126n.146, 130n.271
Monarchy, 89-90
Money, new government-issued, advocated by Robertson, 80-81
Moody Bible Institute, 114
Moody, Dwight L., 114
Moravian Pietism, 111
Mormon church, 7, 25, 60
Mormon Experience, The (Leonard Arrington and Davis Bitton), 126n.145
Moses, 12, 20, 40, 44, 46, 47, 56, 57, 66, 98
Munzerites, 110
Murray, Andrew, 114
My Prayer For You (Pat Robertson), 1, 16
Mysticism, 111, 120

Naboth, 89
National debt, 95; repudiation of, advocated by Robertson, 80-83
National Freedom Institute, 4
National Legal Foundation, 4
National Perspectives Institute, 4
National Religious Broadcasters, 1
Natural law, 71
Nature, 72

Nazism, 87
Neo-orthodoxy, 97
New Age movement, 52
New birth, 2, 14, 23, 74; *see also* Regeneration
New Charismatics, The (Richard Quebedeaux), 126n.142
New Covenant, 119, 131n.279, n.284
New Schaff-Herzog Encyclopedia of Religious Knowledge, The, 60
New Testament, 13
New York Theological Seminary, 1, 3
New York Times, The, 4, 122n.8
New World Order, 85-86
Nicaragua, 87
Nicene and Post-Nicene Fathers, The, 126n.143
Nicodemus, 97, 99
Nietzsche, Friedrich, 97
Noah, 66
Nolen, William, 40-41, 44; Works: *Healing: A Doctor in Search of a Miracle,* 41
North, Gary, 129n.226
Notre Dame University, 118

O'Connor, Edward, 118; Works: *The Pentecostal Movement in the Catholic Church,* 131n.282; *Pentecost in the Catholic Church,* 131n.283
On Religion: Speeches to Its Cultured Despisers (Friedrich Schleiermacher), 130n.257
Oracles, Greek, 60
Oral Roberts University, 1
Original sin, 70-71
Osiander, Andreas, 110

Papacy, 120-121
Parham, Charles, 115
Pat Robertson's Perspective, 34, 36, 79, 124n.67, n.68, n.69, n.70, n.73
Paul, 10, 18, 19, 20, 21, 42, 46, 49, 51, 52, 54, 55, 59, 66, 70, 71, 72, 74, 78, 98, 101, 112
Peale, Norman Vincent, 97
Pelagius, 70
Penance, 119
Pensions, 81
Pentecost, 42
Pentecost in the Catholic Church (Edward O'Connor), 131n.283
Pentecostal Movement in the Catholic Church (Edward O'Connor), 131n.282
Pentecostal movement, 115-116
People for the American Way, 77
Perfectionism, 110, 111-112, 114
Peter, 10-11, 18, 22, 42, 52
Pharaoh, 47
Pharisees, 102, 103
Phi Beta Kappa, xi, 2, 26
Pietism, 110-111
Pilgrims, 85
Plain Account of Christian Perfection, A (John Wesley), 130n.276
Plato, 9
Platonism, 9
Politics, role of Christians in, 80
Politics, Robertson's view, 76-95
Population, 85
Positive Confession, recommended by Robertson, 50-53
Positivism, 97
Power Evangelism (John Wimber,

with Kevin Springer), 98, 130n.260, n.265
Pragmatism, 97
Prayer, 42, 43
Prayer cloths, Robertson's endorsement of, 50
Predestination, 73-74
Present Truth, 130n.274
Presidential Task Force on Victims of Crime, 1
Princeton Theological Seminary, 7, 100
Private interpretation, right denied by Charismatics and Roman Catholics, 78
Proctor, William, 122n.17
Property redistribution of, advocated by Robertson, 80-83, 91-95
Prophecy, xii, 10, 11, 20, 59, 65, 120-121; cessation of, 54-58; Mormon belief in, 60
"Prophetic Authority in the Charismatic Setting: The Need to Test," (Cecil M. Robeck, Jr.), 128n.214
Prophets, false, 24, 32-34, 45, 46
Prophets, testing of, xii, 31-38, 78
"Protestantism, the Pentecostal Movement, and the Drift Back to Rome," 130n.274
PTL Club, xii, 28, 77
Public education, 94-95; supported by Robertson, 80
Puritans, 6
Pursuit of Power: Dominion Theology and the Reconstruction Movement, The (John W. Robbins), 130n.251

Quebedeaux, Richard, 59; *Works:* *The New Charismatics II,* 126n.142

Radio Corporation of America, 27, 76
Raising people from the dead, Robertson's attempt, 44
Reagan, Ronald, 107
Reason, 96-105
Reconstruction movement, 81, 130n.251
Redistribution of property, 91-92, 95; advocated by Robertson, 80-83
Reformation, 6, 7, 12, 13, 109-111, 116-117, 119, 120-121
Reformed Doctrine of Predestination, The (Loraine Boettner), 123n.23
Reformers, 6
Regeneration, 19, 74; *see also* New birth
Reid, T.R., *Works:* "Robertson's Bid Powered by Faith, Self-Assurance," *The Washington Post,* 122n.6
Reincarnation, 8
Relics, 49-50
Religion in Media, 1
Religion, dangers of, 95; as feeling, 96-97
Religious experience, 2, 3, 14, 15, 16, 17
Republic, 89-90
Republican National Committee, 107
Restitution, 88
Resurrection, 98-100
Revelation, 9-13; adding to forbidden, 24; false, 25-38;

Mormon belief in continuing, 60; oral, 11-13, 25-38; written, 10-11
Revivalism, 112-114, 115-116
Righteousness, of Christ, 7, 14; imputed to believers, 110
Robber barons, 83
Robbins, John W., xii; *Works: War and Peace: A Christian Foreign Policy,* 129n.238; *The Pursuit of Power: Dominion Theology and the Reconstruction Movement,* 130n.251
Robeck, Cecil M., Jr., 77; *Works: Charismatic Experiences in History,* 126n.147; "Prophetic Authority in the Charismatic Setting: The Need to Test," 128n.214, 129n.215
Roberts, Oral, xii
Robertson, A. Willis, 1, 2, 26, 79
Robertson, Adelia (Dede) Elmer, 1, 3, 31, 63
Robertson, Ann, 1
Robertson, Elizabeth, 1
Robertson, Gladys Churchill, 1
Robertson, Gordon, 1
Robertson, Pat, *Works: America's Dates With Destiny,* 122n.2, n.3, n.7; *Answers to 200 of Life's Most Probing Questions,* 124n.54, n.55, n.62, 126n.132, 127n.155, n.156, n.157, n.158, n.171, n.172, n.173, n.174, n.175, n.176, 128n.184, n.185, n.188, n.192, n.193, n.194, n.201, n.202, n.208, n.209, 129n.230, n.231, n.232, n.236, n.242, 130n.252, n.272; *Beyond Reason: How Miracles Can Change Your Life,* 122n.17, 123n.47, 124n.81, 125n.82, n.83, n.87, n.92, n.94, n.95, n.96, 126n.127, n.130; "Dictatorships and Single Standards," 129n.239, n.240, n.241; *The Secret Kingdom,* 123n.43, n.44, n.46, n.48, 124n.56, 125n.88, n.89, n.90, n.91, n.93, 126n.118, n.119, n.120, n.125, n.128, n.129, n.131, n.133, n.134, 127n.168, 129n.219, n.220, n.228, n.233, n.234, n.235, n.248; *Shout It From The Housetops,* 122n.4, n.5, 124n.49, n.50, n.51, n.53, n.57, n.58, n.59, n.60, n.61, 126n.136, 127n.149, n.150, n.151, n.152, n.153, n.154, 130n.173; "Toward a Community of Democratic Nations," 129n.237
Robertson, Timothy, 1
"Robertson's Holy Crusade," (Robert Walters), 128n.210, n.213
Rockefellers, 83
Roman Catholic church, 6, 7, 12, 25, 49-50, 77, 78, 114, 116-117
Roman Catholicism (Loraine Boettner), 122n.16
Romantic movement, 97
Russia, *see* Soviet Union

Sabbath, 102
Sadducees, 98-100, 101
Saints, veneration of, 6
Salvation, 7, 10, 14, 19, 25; by works, 74-75
Samuel, 89
Sanctification, 19, 112
Satan, 3, 10, 15, 21, 22, 30, 31, 44-47, 51, 64, 69, 71, 91, 102-103, 104; voice of, 29

Saul, 64
Schleiermacher, Friedrich, 96-97; *Works: On Religion: Speeches to Its Cultured Despisers,* 130n.257
Scientific method, 124n.64
Scriptures, *see* Bible
Second blessing, 113-114
Second Coming of Christ, 14, 19, 23, 36-37, 56
Secret Kingdom, The (Pat Robertson), 1, 5, 16, 123n.43, n.44, n.46, n.48, 124n.56, 125n.88, n.89, n.90, n.91, n.93, 126n.118, n.119, n.120, n.125, n.128, n.129, n.131, n.133, n.134, 127n.168, 129n.219, n.220, n.228, n.233, n.234, n.235, n.248
700 Club, The, 1, 4, 28, 42, 124n.76, 129n.224, n.249
Shamanism, 59, 60
Sherrill, John L., *Works: They Speak With Other Tongues,* 97, 117, 130n.258, n.259
Shout It From The Housetops (Pat Robertson with Jamie Buckingham), 1, 16, 30, 33n.-34n., 54, 122n.4, n.5, 124n.49, n.50, n.51, n.53, n.57, n.58, n.59, n.60, n.61, 126n.136, 127n.149, n.150, n.151, n.152, n.153, n.154, 130n.173
Sider, Ronald, 129n.226
Signs, *see* Miracles
Silas, 78
Simon the sorcerer, 48
Simpson, A.B., 114
Sin, 18n.-19n., 29, 69
Smith, Adam, 83
Smith, Hannah Whitall, *Works: The Christian's Secret of a Happy Life,* 114
Social gospel, 17
Socialism, 83
Socinians, 100
Sola fide, 7, 14, 74
Sola gratia, 7, 74
Sola scriptura, 7, 14, 74
Solomon, 51
Solus Christus, 7, 74
"Something Unusual," (Raymond Frame), 130n.271
Sorcery, 53
South Yemen, 36
Southern Baptist Church, 1, 3
Southern California Motion Picture Council, 1
Soviet Union, 33, 35, 36
"Speaking in Tongues," *The New Schaff-Herzog Encyclopedia of Religious Knowledge,* 126n.144
Spirit and Forms of Protestantism, The (Louis Bouyer), 131n.280
Spirit-Filled Life, The, 114
Spiritism, uses name "Jesus Christ," 60
Spurgeon, Charles Haddon, 106
Stalin, Joseph, 86
Stevenson, Adlai, 2, 79
Stock market crash of 1987, not predicted by Robertson, 35
Stock market crash of 1969, falsely predicted by Robertson's voices, 26
Subba Rao, 60
Subjectivism, 114, 120
Suffering, 51-52, 71, 72
Synan, Vinson, 113; *Works: The Holiness-Pentecostal Movement in the United States,* 131n.277

Taking, by government, 89-90

Technology, Robertson's views on, 85
Ten Commandments, 82, 88
Testing prophets, xii, 31-38, 78
Theological Renewal, 128n.214
Theology of the Holy Spirit, A (Frederick Dale Bruner), 130n.269, 131n.278
They Speak With Other Tongues (John L. Sherrill), 97, 117, 130n.258, n.259
Tillich, Paul, 116-117; *Works: A History of Christian Thought*, 131n.281
Timothy, 10, 49
Tirupathi Venkateswara, 60
Tongues, 14, 16, 59, 65, 115; Biblical meaning of, 61-62; cessation of, 54-58; Mormon belief in, 60
Torrey, R.A., 114
Total depravity, 70
"Toward a Community of Democratic Nations," (Pat Robertson), 86-87, 129n.237
Tradition, 12, 25
Transubstantiation, 119
Trinity, 7, 101
Truth, 10, 14, 20-21, 16, 23, 62, 96

Unification church, 25
Union Theological Seminary, 117, 119
United Nations, 87-88
United States Marine Corps, 1
United Virginia Bank, 1
Universal military training, advocated by Robertson, 88
University of London, 2, 106-107
U.S. Congress, 13, 39, 67, 79

U.S. Constitution, 13, 79, 84
U.S. House of Representatives, 2
U.S. News and World Report, 129n.218

Valencia, Council of, 12
Van Dusen, Henry, 117, 119
Vanderbilts, 83
Vanderbreggen, Cornelius, 2
Victorious Life, The, 114
Viet Cong, 92
Vietnam War, 92
Virgil, *Works: Aeneid*, 59-60
Virgin of Guadalupe, 60
Virginia State Senate, 2
Visions, Mormon belief in, 60
Voices, xi, xii, 5, 11, 12, 16, 24-38, 56, 64, 77, 80, 83, 106-107, 108; of Satan, 29
Voodoo, 60

Wall Street Journal, The, 5, 36, 124n.77, 129n.223
Walters, Robert, *Works:* "Robertson's Holy Crusade," 128n.210, n.213
War, 95, 107; inaccurately predicted by Robertson, 35-36
War and Peace: A Christian Foreign Policy (John W. Robbins), 129n.238
Warfield, Benjamin, *Works: Counterfeit Miracles*, 125n.113, n.114, n.116; *The Westminster Assembly and Its Work*, 100-101, 130n.266
Washington, George, 6, 18
Washington and Lee University, 1, 2
Washington Post, The, 5, 122n.6
Wealth, redistribution of,

advocated by Robertson, 80-83
Weather, Robertson's power over, 43-44, 53
Wesley, John, 111-112, 115; Works: *A Plain Account of Christian Perfection*, 130n.276
Wesleyanism, 111-112, 113
Westminster Assembly and Its Work, The (Benjamin Warfield), 100-101, 130n.266
Westminster Confession of Faith, The, 8, 9, 11, 25, 68, 82, 100-101, 110, 123n.41, 129n.227
What Luther Says (Martin Luther), 130n.275
What Do Presbyterians Believe? (Gordon H. Clark), 9
White, Dick, 31
Whitefield, George, 111-112
Who's Who in America, 1984-1985, 1, 122n.1

Wilkerson, David, 33
Wilson, Woodrow, 87
Wimber, John, 100; *Works: Power Evangelism*, 98, 130n.260, n.265
Wisdom, 26
Wonders, *see* Miracles
Word of knowledge, 27, 65; cessation of, 54-58
Word of wisdom, 26
World War I, 87
World War II, 35
Worship, 30-31
W.R. Grace Company, 1, 2
WTFC, 29
WYAH, 29

Yale University Law School, xi, 1, 26, 84
Young, Brigham, 60

Zacchaeus, 89

The Crisis of Our Time

Historians have christened the thirteenth century the Age of Faith and termed the eighteenth century the Age of Reason. The twentieth century has been called many things: the Atomic Age, the Age of Inflation, the Age of the Tyrant, the Age of Aquarius. But it deserves one name more than the others: the Age of Irrationalism. Contemporary secular intellectuals are anti-intellectual. Contemporary philosophers are anti-philosophy. Contemporary theologians are anti-theology.

In past centuries secular philosophers have generally believed that knowledge is possible to man. Consequently they expended a great deal of thought and effort trying to justify knowledge. In the twentieth century, however, the optimism of the secular philosophers has all but disappeared. They despair of knowledge.

Like their secular counterparts, the great theologians and doctors of the church taught that knowledge is possible to man. Yet the theologians of the twentieth century have repudiated that belief. They also despair of knowledge. This radical skepticism has filtered down from the philosophers and theologians and penetrated our entire culture, from television to music to literature. *The Christian in the twentieth century is confronted with an overwhelming cultural consensus—sometimes stated explicitly, but most often implicitly: Man does not and cannot know anything truly.*

What does this have to do with Christianity? Simply this: If man can know nothing truly, man can truly know nothing. We cannot know that the Bible is the Word of God, that Christ died for sin, or that Christ is alive today at the right hand of the Father. Unless knowledge is possible, Christianity is nonsensical, for it claims to be knowledge. What is at stake in the twentieth century is not simply a single doctrine, such as the Virgin Birth, or the existence of hell, as important as those doctrines may be, but the whole of Christianity itself. If knowledge is not possible to man, it is worse than silly to argue points of doctrine—it is insane.

The irrationalism of the present age is so thorough-going and pervasive that even the Remnant—the segment of the professing church that remains faithful—has accepted much of it, frequently without even being aware of what it was accepting. In some circles this irrationalism has become synonymous with piety and humility, and those who oppose it are denounced as rationalists—as though to be logical were a sin. Our contemporary anti-theologians make a contradiction and call it a Mystery. The faithful ask for truth and are given Paradox. If any balk at swallowing the absurdities of the anti-theologians, they are frequently marked as heretics or schismatics who seek to act independently of God.

There is no greater threat facing the true Church of Christ at this moment than the irrationalism that now controls our entire culture. Communism, guilty of tens of millions of murders, including those of millions of Christians, is to be feared, but not nearly so much as the idea that we do not and cannot know the truth. Hedonism, the popular philosophy of America, is not to be feared so much as the belief that logic—that "mere human logic," to use the religious irrationalists' own phrase—is futile. The attacks on truth, on revelation, on the intellect, and on logic are renewed daily. But note well: The misologists—the haters of logic—use logic to demonstrate the futility of using logic. The anti-intellectuals construct intricate intellectual arguments to prove the insufficiency of the intellect. The anti-theologians use the revealed Word of God to show that there can be no revealed Word of God—or that if there could, it would remain impenetrable darkness and Mystery to our finite minds.

Nonsense Has Come

Is it any wonder that the world is grasping at straws—the straws of experientialism, mysticism and drugs? After all, if people are told that the Bible contains insoluble mysteries, then is not a flight into mysticism to be expected? On what grounds can it be condemned? Certainly not on logical grounds or Biblical grounds, if logic is futile and the Bible unintelligible. Moreover, if it cannot be condemned on logical or Biblical grounds, it cannot be condemned at all. If people are going to have a religion of the mysterious, they will not adopt Christianity: They will have a genuine mystery religion. "Those who call for Nonsense," C.S. Lewis once wrote, "will find that it comes." And that is precisely what has happened. The popularity of Eastern mysticism, of drugs, and of religious experience is the logical consequence of the irrationalism of the twentieth century. There can and will be no Christian revival—and no reconstruction of society—unless and until the irrationalism of the age is totally repudiated by Christians.

The Church Defenseless

Yet how shall they do it? The spokesmen for Christianity have been fatally infected with irrationalism. The seminaries, which annually train thousands of men to teach millions of Christians, are the finishing schools of irrationalism, completing the job begun by the government schools and colleges. Some of the pulpits of the most conservative churches (we are not speaking of the apostate churches) are occupied by graduates of the anti-theological schools. These products of modern anti-theological education, when asked to give a reason for the hope that is in them, can generally respond with only the intellectual analogue of a shrug—a mumble about Mystery. They have not grasped—and therefore cannot teach those for whom they are responsible—the first truth: "And ye shall know the truth." Many, in fact, explicitly deny it, saying that, at best, we possess only "pointers" to the truth, or something "similar" to the truth, a mere analogy. Is the impotence of the Christian Church a puzzle? Is the fascination with pentecostalism and faith healing among members of conservative churches an enigma? Not when one understands the sort of studied nonsense that is purveyed in the name of God in the seminaries.

The Trinity Foundation

The creators of The Trinity Foundation firmly believe that theology is too important to be left to the licensed theologians —the graduates of the schools of theology. They have created The Trinity Foundation for the express purpose of teaching the faithful all that the Scriptures contain—not warmed over, baptized, secular philosophies. Each member of the board of directors of The Trinity Foundation has signed this oath: "I believe that the Bible alone and the Bible in its entirety is the Word of God and, therefore, inerrant in the autographs. I believe that the system of truth presented in the Bible is best summarized in the Westminster Confession of Faith. So help me God."

The ministry of The Trinity Foundation is the presentation of the system of truth taught in Scripture as clearly and as completely as possible. We do not regard obscurity as a virtue, nor confusion as a sign of spirituality. Confusion, like all error, is sin, and teaching that confusion is all that Christians can hope for is doubly sin.

The presentation of the truth of Scripture necessarily involves the rejection of error. The Foundation has exposed and will continue to expose the irrationalism of the twentieth century, whether its current spokesman be an existentialist philosopher or a professed Reformed theologian. We oppose anti-intellectualism, whether it be espoused by a neo-orthodox theologian or a fundamentalist evangelist. We reject misology, whether it be on the lips of a neo-evangelical or those of a Roman Catholic charismatic. To each error we bring the brilliant light of Scripture, proving all things, and holding fast to that which is true.

The Primacy of Theory

The ministry of The Trinity Foundation is not a "practical" ministry. If you are a pastor, we will not enlighten you on how to organize an ecumenical prayer meeting in your community or how to double church attendance in a year. If you are a homemaker, you will have to read elsewhere to find out how to become a total woman. If you are a businessman, we will not tell you how to develop a social conscience. The professing church is drowning in such "practical" advice.

The Trinity Foundation is unapologetically theoretical in its outlook, believing that theory without practice is dead, and that practice without theory is blind. The trouble with the professing church is not primarily in its practice, but in its theory. Christians do not know, and many do not even care to know, the doctrines of Scripture. Doctrine is intellectual, and Christians are generally anti-intellectual. Doctrine is ivory tower philosophy, and they scorn ivory towers. The ivory tower, however, is the control tower of a civilization. It is a fundamental, theoretical mistake of the practical men to think that they can be merely practical, for practice is always the practice of some theory. The relationship between theory and practice is the relationship between cause and effect. If a person believes correct theory, his practice will tend to be correct. The practice of contemporary Christians is immoral because it is the practice of false theories. It is a major theoretical mistake of the practical men to think that they can ignore the ivory towers of the philosophers and theologians as irrelevant to their lives. Every action that the "practical" men take is governed by the thinking that has occurred in some ivory tower—whether that tower be the British Museum, the Academy, a home in Basel, Switzerland, or a tent in Israel.

In Understanding Be Men

It is the first duty of the Christian to understand correct theory—correct doctrine—and thereby implement correct practice. This order—first theory, then practice—is both logical and Biblical. It is, for example, exhibited in Paul's epistle to the Romans, in which he spends the first eleven chapters expounding theory and the last five discussing practice. The contemporary teachers of Christians have not only reversed the order, they have inverted the Pauline emphasis on theory and practice. The virtually complete failure of the teachers of the professing church to instruct the faithful in correct doctrine is the cause of the misconduct and cultural impotence of Christians. The Church's lack of power is the result of its lack of truth. The *Gospel* is the power of God, not religious experience or personal relationship. The Church has no power because it has abandoned the Gospel, the good news, for a religion of experientialism. Twentieth century American Christians are children carried about by every wind of doctrine, not knowing what they believe, or even if they believe anything for certain.

The chief purpose of The Trinity Foundation is to counteract the irrationalism of the age and to expose the errors of the teachers of the church. Our emphasis—on the Bible as the sole source of truth, on the primacy of the intellect, on the supreme importance of correct doctrine, and on the necessity for systematic and logical thinking—is almost unique in Christendom. To the extent that the church survives—and she will survive and flourish—it will be because of her increasing acceptance of these basic ideas and their logical implications.

We believe that the Trinity Foundation is filling a vacuum in Christendom. We are saying that Christianity is intellectually defensible—that, in fact, it is the only intellectually defensible system of thought. We are saying that God has made the wisdom of this world—whether that wisdom be called science, religion, philosophy, or common sense—foolishness. We are appealing to all Christians who have not conceded defeat in the intellectual battle with the world to join us in our efforts to raise a standard to which all men of sound mind can repair.

The love of truth, of God's Word, has all but disappeared in our time. We are committed to and pray for a great instauration. But though we may not see this reformation of Christendom in our lifetimes, we believe it is our duty to present the whole counsel of God because Christ has commanded it. The results of our teaching are in God's hands, not ours. Whatever those results, His Word is never taught in vain, but always accomplishes the result that He intended it to accomplish. Professor Gordon H. Clark has stated our view well:

> There have been times in the history of God's people, for example, in the days of Jeremiah, when refreshing grace and widespread revival were not to be expected: the time was one of chastisement. If this twentieth century is of a similar nature, individual Christians here and there can find comfort and strength in a study of God's Word. But if God has decreed happier days for us and if we may expect a world-shaking and genuine spiritual awakening, then it is the author's belief that a zeal for souls, however necessary, is not the sufficient condition. Have there not been devout saints in every age, numerous enough to carry on a revival? Twelve such persons are plenty. What distinguishes the arid ages from the period of the Reformation, when nations were moved as they had not been since Paul preached in Ephesus, Corinth, and Rome, is the latter's fullness of knowledge of God's Word. To echo an early Reformation thought, when the ploughman and the garage attendant know the Bible as well as the theologian does, and know it better than some contemporary theologians, then the desired awakening shall have already occurred.

In addition to publishing books, of which *Pat Robertson: A Warning to America* is the twenty-fourth, the Foundation publishes a bimonthly newsletter, *The Trinity Review*. Subscriptions to *The Review* are free; please write to the address below to become a subscriber. If you would like further information or would like to join us in our work, please let us know.

The Trinity Foundation is a non-profit foundation tax-exempt under section 501 (c)(3) of the Internal Revenue Code of 1954. You can help us disseminate the Word of God through your tax-deductible contributions to the Foundation.

And we know that the Son of God is come, and hath given us an understanding, that we may know him that is true, and we are in him that is true, in his Son Jesus Christ. This is the true God, and eternal life.

John W. Robbins
President

Intellectual Ammunition

The Trinity Foundation is committed to the reconstruction of philosophy and theology along Biblical lines. We regard God's command to bring all our thoughts into conformity with Christ very seriously, and the books listed below are designed to accomplish that goal. They are written with two subordinate purposes: (1) to demolish all secular claims to knowledge; and (2) to build a system of truth based upon the Bible alone.

Works of Philosophy

Answer to Ayn Rand, John W. Robbins $4.95
  The only analysis and criticism of the views of novelist-philosopher Ayn Rand from a consistently Christian perspective.

Behaviorism and Christianity, Gordon H. Clark $5.95
  Behaviorism *is a critique of both secular and religious behaviorists. It includes chapters on John Watson, Edgar S. Singer Jr., Gilbert Ryle, B.F. Skinner, and Donald MacKay. Clark's refutation of behaviorism and his argument for a Christian doctrine of man are unanswerable.*

A Christian Philosophy of Education, Gordon H. Clark $8.95
  The first edition of this book was published in 1946. It sparked the contemporary interest in Christian schools. Dr. Clark has thoroughly revised and updated it, and it is needed now more than ever. Its chapters include: The Need for a World-View, The Christian World-View, The

Alternative to Christian Theism, Neutrality, Ethics, The Christian Philosophy of Education, Academic Matters, Kindergarten to University. Three appendices are included as well: The Relationship of Public Education to Christianity, A Protestant World-View, and Art and the Gospel.

A Christian View of Men and Things, Gordon H. Clark $8.95
No other book achieves what A Christian View *does: the presentation of Christianity as it applies to history, politics, ethics, science, religion, and epistemology. Clark's command of both worldly philosophy and Scripture is evident on every page, and the result is a breathtaking and invigorating challenge to the wisdom of this world.*

Clark Speaks From The Grave, Gordon H. Clark $3.95
Dr. Clark chides some of his critics for their failure to defend Christianity competently. Clark Speaks *is a stimulating and illuminating discussion of the errors of contemporary apologists.*

Education, Christianity, and the State $7.95
J. Gresham Machen
This is the only collection of Machen's nine essays on Christian scholarship and education. Machen was one of the foremost educators of the twentieth century, and his defense of Christian education and intellectual freedom is even more timely now than it was 50 years ago.

John Dewey, Gordon H. Clark $2.00
Dewey has had an immense influence on American philosophy and education. His irrationalism, the effects of which we can see in government education, is thoroughly critized by Dr. Clark.

Logic, Gordon H. Clark $8.95
Written as a textbook for Christian schools, Logic *is another unique book from Clark's pen. His presentation of the laws of thought, which must be followed if Scripture is to be understood correctly, and which are found in Scripture itself, is both clear and thorough.* Logic *is an indispensable book for the thinking Christian.*

The Philosophy of Science and Belief in God $5.95
Gordon H. Clark
In opposing the contemporary idolatry of science, Clark analyzes three major aspects of science: the problem of motion, Newtonian science, and modern theories of physics. His conclusion is that science, while it may be useful, is always false; and he demonstrates its falsity in numerous ways. Since science is always false, it can offer no objection to the Bible and Christianity.

Religion, Reason and Revelation, Gordon H. Clark $7.95
One of Clark's apologetical masterpieces, Religion, Reason and Revelation *has been praised for the clarity of its thought and language. It includes chapters on Is Christianity a Religion? Faith and Reason, Inspiration and Language, Revelation and Morality, and God and Evil. It is must reading for all serious Christians.*

Selections from Hellenistic Philosophy, Gordon H. Clark $10.95
Early in his academic career Clark translated, edited, and commented upon the writings of several philosophers: Lucretius, Zeno of Citium, Chrysippus, Plutarch, Philo Judaeus, Hermes Trismegistus, and Plotinus.

Works of Theology

The Atonement, Gordon H. Clark $8.95
This is a major addition to Clark's multi-volume systematic theology. In The Atonement, *Clark discusses the Covenants, the Virgin Birth and Incarnation, federal headship and representation, the relationship between God's sovereignty and justice, and much more. He analyzes traditional views of the Atonement and criticizes them in the light of Scripture alone.*

The Biblical Doctrine of Man, Gordon H. Clark $5.95
Is man soul and body or soul, spirit, and body? What is the image of God? Is Adam's sin imputed to his children? Is evolution true? Are men totally depraved? What is the heart? These are some to the questions discussed and answered from Scripture in this book.

Cornelius Van Til: The Man and The Myth $2.45
John W. Robbins
The actual teachings of this eminent Philadelphia theologian have been obscured by the myths that surround him. This book penetrates those myths and criticizes Van Til's surprisingly unorthodox views of God and the Bible.

Faith and Saving Faith, Gordon H. Clark $5.95
The views of the Roman Catholic church, John Calvin, Thomas Manton, John Owen, Charles Hodge, and B.B. Warfield are discussed in this book. Is the object of faith a person or a proposition? Is faith more than belief? Is belief more than thinking with assent, as Augustine said? In a world chaotic with differing views of faith, Clark clearly explains the Biblical view of faith and saving faith.

God's Hammer: The Bible and Its Critics, Gordon H. Clark $6.95
The starting point of Christianity, the doctrine on which all other doctrines depend, is "The Bible is the Word of God, and therefore inerrant in the autographs." Over the centuries the opponents of Christianity, with Satanic shrewdness, have concentrated their attacks on the truthfulness of the Bible. In the twentieth century the attack is not so much in the fields of history and archaeology as in philosophy. Clark's brilliant defense of the complete truthfulness of the Bible is captured in this collection of eleven major essays.

In Defense of Theology, Gordon H. Clark $12.95
There are four groups to whom Clark addresses this book: the average Christians who are uninterested in theology, the atheists and agnostics, the religious experientialists, and the serious Christians. The vindication of the knowledge of God against the objections of three of these groups is the first step in theology.

Logical Criticisms of Textual Criticism, Gordon H. Clark $2.95
In this critique of the science of textual criticism, Dr. Clark exposes the fallacious argumentation of the modern textual critics and defends the view that the early Christians knew better than the modern critics which manuscripts of the New Testament were more accurate.

Pat Robertson: A Warning to America, John W. Robbins $6.95
The Protestant Reformation was based on the Biblical principle that the Bible is the only revelation from God, yet a growing political- religious movement, led by Pat Robertson, asserts that God speaks to them directly. This book addresses the serious issue of religious fanaticism in America by examining the theological and political views of Presidential candidate Pat Robertson.

Predestination, Gordon H. Clark $7.95
Clark thoroughly discusses one of the most controversial and pervasive doctrines of the Bible: that God is, quite literally, Almighty. Free will, the origin of evil, God's omniscience, creation, and the new birth are all presented within a Scriptural framework. The objections of those who do not believe in the Almighty God are considered and refuted. This volume contains the texts of Biblical Predestination *and* Predestination in the Old Testament.

Scripture Twisting in the Seminaries. Part 1: Feminism $5.95
John W. Robbins
An analysis of the views of three graduates of Westminster Seminary on the role of women in the church.

The Trinity, Gordon H. Clark $8.95
Apart from the doctrine of Scripture, no teaching of the Bible is more important than the doctrine of God. Clark's defense of the orthodox doctrine of the Trinity is a principal portion of a major new work of Systematic Theology now in progress. There are chapters on the deity of Christ, Augustine, the incomprehensibility of God, Bavinck and Van Til, and the Holy Spirit, among others.

What Do Presbyterians Believe? Gordon H. Clark $6.95
This classic introduction to Christian doctrine has been republished. It is the best commentary on the Westminster Confession of Faith that has ever been written.

Commentaries on the New Testament

Ephesians, Gordon H. Clark	$8.95
First and Second Thessalonians, Gordon H. Clark	$5.95
The Pastoral Epistles (I and II Timothy and Titus) Gordon H. Clark	$9.95

All of Clark's commentaries are expository, not technical, and are written for the Christian layman. His purpose is to explain the text clearly and accurately so that the Word of God will be thoroughly known by every Christian. Revivals of Christianity come only through the spread of God's truth. The sound exposition of the Bible, through preaching and through commentaries on Scripture, is the only method of spreading that truth.

The Trinity Library

We will send you one copy of each of the 26 books listed above for the low price of $125. The regular price of these books is $175. Or you may order the books you want individually on the order blank at the back. Because some of the books are in short supply, we must reserve the right to substitute others of equal or greater value in The Trinity Library.

Thank you for your attention. We hope to hear from you soon. This special offer expires June 30, 1989.

Order Form

Name _____

Address _____

_____

Please: ☐ add my name to the mailing list for *The Trinity Review.* I understand that there is no charge for the *Review.*

☐ accept my tax deductible contribution of $ _____ for the work of the Foundation.

☐ send me _____ copies of *Pat Robertson: A Warning to America.* I enclose as payment $ _____.

☐ send me the Trinity Library of 26 books. I enclose $125 as full payment for it.

☐ send me the following books. I enclose full payment in the amount of $ _____ for them.

_____

_____

_____

_____

_____

_____

_____

Mail to: The Trinity Foundation
Post Office Box 169
Jefferson, MD 21755

Please add $1.00 for postage on orders less than $10. Thank you.
For quantity discounts, please write to the Foundation.